THE
INVISIBLE
WOMEN

ADDRESSING THE INTERSECTION OF PAY AND RACISM IN THE WORKPLACE

MELODY SIMMONS-HUDSON
MONICA SIMMONS

13TH & JOAN

The Invisible Women. Copyright 2022 by Melody Simmons-Hudson and Monica Simmons. All rights reserved. No part of this publication may be reproduced, distributed, or transmitted in any form or by any means, including photocopying, recording, or other electronic or mechanical methods, without the prior written permission of the publisher, except in the case of brief quotations embodied in critical reviews and certain other noncommercial uses permitted by copyright law.

For permission requests, write to the publisher, addressed "Attention: Permissions Coordinator," 205 N. Michigan Avenue, Suite #810, Chicago, IL 60601. 13th & Joan books may be purchased for educational, business or sales promotional use. For information, please email the Sales Department at sales@13thandjoan.com.

Printed in the U. S. A.

First Printing, October 2022.

Library of Congress Cataloging-in-Publication Data has been applied for.

ISBN: 978-1-953156-87-7

Monica
*To our mother and father for instilling in us since we were children to
be bold, to speak up, and to empower other little girls and ourselves.*

Melody
*To my daughter, Chloe Hudson, who has always been supportive of
her mom doing all of this work for the past six years. Having you
in my life is such a blessing . Please use this torch to light your path
forward, as you continue walking into your destiny for greatness.*

*To all the strong women in my family: The matriarchs, my
sister, and all the women and girls I have been able to work
with along this path. To those who have empowered me, given
me confidence, and the inspiration to build a platform.*

FOREWORD

In our weakest times are the moments we discover just how much strength we actually have. The world may view you as "invisible," but my daughters, continue to stand strong, pull from your God-given power within, and never dim your light.

During my time in the early 1980s and 1990s, many women like myself didn't have the tools and resources readily available to tackle the obstacles and barriers faced in the workplace, especially in corporate America. Racism, sexism, ageism, and even colorism were daily battles for Black women. I remember walking into the workplace during my career in Silicon Valley, which mainly consisted of whites. Because of my fairer skin, many bosses and co-workers viewed me as ambiguous. As a Black woman from the Midwest, never did I waiver on my blackness. I stood strong on the principles I learned growing up from the bold, driven, and successful women around me. It was instilled in me early on that "If you don't stand for something, you'll fall for anything." These same sets of morals and values I hope to pass on to you during your journey, and I am so proud of the path forward you all are setting for generations to come.

No longer should Black women have to be seen and unheard or feel compelled to code-switch in order to be accepted, but rather hold true to their authentic selves in all of their greatness. I made the hard decision to leave corporate America after feeling time and time again the pressure to choose between career and family and being passed over and over for promotions after working hard to be noticed.

My hope was always for my daughters and grandchildren to go further than me. Take the torch and continue to blaze trails for women and families that are often overlooked.

Princess Simmons (mother),

ACKNOWLEDGMENTS

MELODY

I would like to express my gratitude to my sister, Monica, for being such a good business partner and coauthor.

Thank you, 13th & Joan Publishing House. You all have been awesome in helping us bring forth this book.

To my family, who has always supported us throughout this journey.

To the women, girls, and allies who have continued to rally us along.

Thankful and grateful to God for the many blessings and for guiding my footsteps throughout this journey. I am nothing without you!

MONICA

I would like to acknowledge my sister, Melody, who has been a great co-author throughout this process.

Thank you to all the women before us who tried for this same cause that we are fighting for. We are not the first to do it and won't be the last.

Gratitude towards Kimberly Crenshaw for coining the term "intersectionality" and Audre Loudre.

INTRODUCTION

MONICA

This book will reveal the experience of the Black woman in the workplace. It is not set on an equal level playing field when it comes to your wages as well as being developed in whatever you are working at. What we are revealing in this book is the discrepancy between the Black woman and other women who are not of color. The experience is so different, but there are things that we can do to better our experiences in the workplace, such as knowing our worth, asking for what we want, advocating for ourselves, and taking charge of our careers. We cannot expect other people to do it, especially when we are working alongside people who have so many biases against women, especially Black women.

MELODY

We are going to touch on the inequities that Black women and women of color experience in the workplace, as well as the power that you truly hold, including how you can overcome those obstacles and be an advocate for yourself, and how you can stay encouraged and motivated on your journey. For Monica and I, through our trials, there were many times when we just wanted to give up and didn't feel like we had a support system to lean on.

We want this book to be a reference guide for you to be able to tap into. Use it to get more clarification on the legal aspects and laws around things that are happening to you and know that there are things that you can do about it. There are resources that you can access. Black women belong at the table where decisions are being made. I want us to continue blazing trails, and taking up space.

CONTENTS

22: Time's Up

222: The Equal Pay Movement *131*

I:
ME TOO

Our Story

"BLACK WOMEN NEED TO
BE VALUED AND RESPECTED
IN THE WORKPLACE."

Melody

Parental separation is something that changes you in a way you're not prepared for, but you still have to accept it and do the best you can with the tools you are given. For me, our parents' separation thrust me into the role of nurturer for my sister Monica. I was about 10 years old, and our mother sent us to live with our grandmother for an academic year. A strong and self-sufficient woman, our mother needed to regroup once the separation birthed into a divorce, and she was left with three girls. Nonetheless, it never stopped me from seeing her as the fantastic wife and goal-getter I knew her to be. Our parents married young but never allowed their age to stop them from attaining great success. They were entrepreneurial, starting businesses and buying properties in the Midwest as well as California, all while raising a family. Despite the change from a two-parent household, our mom gave us all the tools we needed to be successful women in our own right. A corporate professional, she knew how to turn oranges into orange trees, even if she only had the peels.

My mother worked as a corporate professional, moving up the management ladder at reputable Fortune 500 companies in Silicon Valley right before the birth of the dot.com era. Unfortunately, the pressures of her divorce and raising three children as a single parent took a heavy toll, and not much grace in the corporate world was afforded to her as a Black woman. Still, she made sure her three girls had everything. She was lovely and, without a doubt, the greatest role model.

As a teenager, my drive to work kicked in early. Our mother would probably describe me as emotionally mature for my age, but I still knew my boundaries as a child. Some may have called kids like me an "old soul." I was motivated to help in whatever way. Raising three children wasn't easy, and though she never put a burden on us to help her, you could feel the financial strain at times. I wanted to help with that. My work ethic was solid. I took on various jobs, such as at the mall and at Burger King, and later I began doing hair for my friends and peers at our kitchen table. This was while I was attending cosmetology school and working toward my diploma. My hope was to one day open my own full-service salon. After doing enough at-home styling, my dream changed. One thing that was always certain for me was following in my mom's footsteps in entrepreneurship. Going into finance became an inevitable goal for me. My mom's influence was strong and guided me as I transitioned into high school.

If I could have, I would've skipped high school and walked straight on to college. I didn't dislike going to school, but getting a taste of working and making money to buy items that weren't a high priority for mama, like "cool clothes and shoes," had me ready to head off to college and prepare for a successful career. During my childhood, seeing people in my family involved in organizations like the NAACP and the Black Caucus helped me understand the importance of representation for Black people. This led to me joining the Black Student Union at my high school and also the Step Team, which kept me connected with my culture. As a young child, I always dreamt of attending a historically Black college or university (HBCU). Attending an HBCU started to become a reality once my childhood friend and a cousin, who was like a sister, got accepted into one and was headed down south. Unfortunately, I encountered a male teacher who was indeed Black but did not see the vision I had.

In his words, *"The world is more than Black people. You need to broaden your perspective."*

He discouraged my plans to head off to Louisiana where my cousin attended. To add fuel to the fire, my cousin tragically passed away. That was a life-changing event that led to my decision to attend college near home. I was a full-time college student and after taking several accounting and finance courses, I soon began to develop a love for working with numbers.

Witnessing a Black woman be a manager at a bank was an epiphany for me. Seeing her made me realize that Black women could indeed be bosses in the world of finance. It was at that moment that I was motivated like never before. I made my plan and pursued my bachelor's degree in business/social sciences and then an MBA in finance, which set the foundation for continuing a career within the finance industry.

Monica

Being the last child of a family comes with a luxury that is unspoken as well as heard. I will admit that I was spoiled, and one thing I could count on was my parents being there and providing me with anything that I needed. The devastating reality of divorce was confusing and painful. I witnessed my family quickly shift, and everything I knew and enjoyed came to a screeching halt. The properties they owned were in jeopardy, and the scariest thing for me was leaving the comfort and life I knew in California for my grandmother's home in Michigan. Michigan lacked the diversity of California, and it was a much different culture than what I was used to. It was a complete culture shock to my young heart and mind. Even our grandmother's house was different. There were multiple people who lived there, and there was never a dull moment between the large family of aunts, uncles, and cousins, as well as neighborhood friends who would visit daily. They all loved my grandmother's warm, inviting spirit and her good cooking. It was the ultimate gathering spot. The shift from being in the home with two parents to my grandmother's house with multiple family members created a feeling of loneliness.

Even though I was still the center of attention at my grandmother's house, I missed my parents and desperately wanted to move back home. After a school year of living with our grandmother, we returned to California, and it was so special because we had everything new. Bunk beds, clothes, toothbrushes with our names on them, toys, bikes–you name it, and we had it! It was Christmas in the summertime.

During my childhood, my mom transitioned careers from corporate America to the medical field so she could become involved with extracurricular activities that she did not have the time for with my older siblings. I was involved in different sports and cheerleading throughout elementary and middle school, as well as ballet and jazz dance, so I had a busy afterschool schedule.

Becoming an entrepreneur was, without a doubt, my destiny. I witnessed the success of both my parents and knew it was the path I was destined to follow. One particular business my mother commanded was going to the homes of individuals who could not drive, drawing their blood for their doctor, and delivering it to the lab. It was significant because I assisted her in that business, and she actually paid me. From there, the entrepreneurial drive took off. While in high school, I started my own fashion business. We attended a private Catholic high school, and I made outfits for the students who were in talent shows or just needed them. It felt good to do it and know people were interested in what I was supplying. Another plus was having uplifting people around me beyond my sisters and parents. While in high school, I kept a group of friends who were inspiring. We shared our dreams and aspirations of what we wanted to do after graduating. I went on after attending a local university earning a degree in Business.

Our Truths

Melody

I first realized racism and ageism in the workplace was a problem very early on in my corporate career. I was around 21 years old and a full-time college student employed by a Fortune 500 company. It was an entry-level position in the billing department of accounting. No matter what position or company I work for, I am always ambitious. I gain as much information as possible to teach myself so that I can excel. I make sure to plan out five to 10 goals on how to build my own career ladder. In this position, there was a new manager who came on board and took a real liking to me. She was a middle-aged caucasian woman who had years of experience. At that moment, she seemed far from a threat or a person who was against me. I actually saw her as a mentor. She was personable and appeared to be a good person and colleague. I trusted her and believed she was another woman in my path who could help me, a Black woman. She gave me a 5-star rating on my performance, and though I was young, she allowed me to lead the department and help with different initiatives. Soon the discussion of planning my promotion to a supervisory position began. We were very open with sharing ideas and conversations on how we were going to continue building out the department and staffing leading up to my transition into a supervisory role. Unbeknownst to me, there were other plans.

A few months into our planning for my future success, a new face arrived in the company–her friend from a previous workplace. All of a sudden, she wanted me to train this friend, who was also an older woman. The woman needed work because she had recently been let go from her job. Naturally, I wanted the whole team to win but also, being young and unaware of the politics of race and ageism hiding in kindness, I didn't think anything of it. I helped her friend. I made sure she had all the information and skills I did. Finally, the supervisory position was posted. My opportunity had arrived. I couldn't wait. It was a position that paid fairly well, and I was eager to have it. Little did I know it was being pulled from my hands right under my nose. During a training session with my supervisor's friend, she casually mentioned to me that she was, in fact, being moved into my anticipated position. I thought she was confused. Was I training her to practice my supervisory skills? There was no way this woman I trained was coming in to steal what I had planned for months. Confused and hurt, to say the least, I asked my manager when I would move into the role. The reality of what she would tell me was more than harsh. While she believed I was a great team player and fantastic for the role, I was too young for such a high position. Her friend, who was older and used to make more money, could in no way be dropped down to a junior-level position. I was flabbergasted. How could women move that way in the workplace? That was the moment I knew there was a problem not only of race but of ageism. We were the same sex, so gender wasn't a factor, but the reality is that white women look out for other women who look like them and Black women like myself are left out. And, to set the record straight, Black women have been "LEANING IN."

Monica

I can remember when I first realized racism was a bigger issue than I originally thought. I entered corporate life in my early 20s. There was a particular time when I was at the mid-senior level. I got a sign-on bonus to join this tech company in San Francisco, a new job, and a new role. I had never received a sign-on bonus before, and this one came as soon as I completed the paperwork. The feeling of accomplishment was undeniable. To place the cherry on top, I received a higher salary for just coming on board. Unfortunately, my feelings of accomplishment were short-lived. The manager who hired me ended up taking another job at a different company and one of my colleagues, who was a peer, moved into a management role. Not even a week after she began, she developed the title "Workplace Karen." Out of the blue, she had an issue with me as soon as she became manager. In no subtle way, she wanted me to know she was the boss. One day she brought the CFO into a meeting with us, and she snapped. Aggressive and hostile, she told me I needed to understand that she was the new manager and I was to do everything she demanded from me. She took pleasure in seeing herself over me but little did she know, no one is over me but God.

Nonetheless, I was taken aback in shock because I thought I was following along with what I was tasked with. I never gave her any pushback, so I was baffled as to where this was all coming from. As time went on, she emailed me certain assignments that were completely unexpected. She instructed me to do a presentation deck for some task I was doing and hand it to her the next morning. She was going to send it over to the founders and CEO, and she laid out everything I was to complete. It was as if she was trying to push my buttons, but I didn't cave that easily. As Black women, we fight through it. We stick to our guns and keep going. We continue to be strong. Some of the other colleagues in cross-functional departments, such as human resources and the deals desk, noticed the awkwardness between her and I.

They asked how things were going. I made sure to be careful with my words. At work, you don't want to speak out of turn, so I was cautious when articulating myself and kept my responses professional yet candid. I told the other managers things were going okay. They knew she was a troublemaker and would tell me to be careful with her. These were other non-Black colleagues telling me to be careful. They knew company-wide that this young lady was a problem child.

The last straw for me was during the final meeting she and I had. I knew it was weird because she scheduled the meeting at 6:30 p.m. Instantly, I knew the troublemaker was coming to set fire. She called me into a conference room after the majority of everyone had left the building. Once I arrived, she went on this tirade. Angry and yelling, she told me I better do everything she said or else. She slammed her hands down on the table and became more aggressive with every word that slithered out of her mouth. I knew that it was safer for me to leave, but as I got up out of my seat, she demanded I sit back down. It was frightening. It was as if horns were coming out of her head. I had no idea where the mountain of animosity was coming from.

As I was getting up from the table, she stood up and yelled: *"No! You sit down right now, and you better not leave. You are going to listen to me. You better sit down right now!"*

I continued to move away from the table, doing my best not to engage. Keeping my words calm, I told her: *"Wait a minute. Back up. I do not have to do anything. I feel uncomfortable."*

Quickly I left the conference room, bursting into tears, but they weren't tears of fear. I instantly knew that my career at this company was over. There was no way I was going to work with this girl again, but who was going to believe me over this white woman explaining a story about aggression and hostility? Even if they did believe me, would they care? If you listen to my story, you know it is obvious racism and nothing else. I did all of my work. I followed all of her directions. Even HR told me I was doing everything right. It was her and not me. The next day when I arrived at work, I talked to the VP. The look on his face showed he believed me, but he didn't do anything about it. He did absolutely nothing. That only solidified what I already came to realize. This lady was super aggressive and was on the verge of getting physical with me, but no one cared. If I had not gotten up, there is no telling what she would have done. At that point, I said, *"No, never again."* I left that role and started to rebuild, but the cracks of the past would haunt me.

Not many years after that experience, something very similar happened. That is when Melody and I knew we had to do something, and that is how our documentary *Invisible Women: Being a Black Woman in Corporate America* was born from our stories and many others. I can remember that particular story like it was yesterday because I could not believe that someone would act that way in a corporate office and think it was okay.

After I moved on to become a manager working at a different company, an ex-coworker of mine began working with the same aggressive, angry manager. When the bad boss looked at her resume, she questioned my former colleague on whether or not she knew me. My ex-coworker confirmed that she did know me and ranted and raved about how good and positive I was and how we were friends. My friend said she thought it was something weird because when the bad boss asked about me, she had a smirk on her face as if my ex-coworker was going to say something negative about me. When she did not, the dreadful manager didn't say anything else. She never ever mentioned me again.

Common Myths

Monica

- **Common Myth:** If you leave your job due to discrimination, you will not find another job or become blackballed from your industry.

- **Truth:** Not only will you find another job, but you will also find your voice so the next time you experience discrimination on the job, you can report it sooner than later.

- **Common Myth:** HR is going to immediately react to your complaint and reprimand the offender.

- **Truth:** There is a long extended process. Initially, HR will react to your report as if it is not true and spend more time investigating you and your work rather than looking into the person you have reported for discrimination.

- **Common Myth:** After you submit your request to HR, you can stay in your role and excel at the company.

- **Truth:** By involving HR, most of the company will be afraid to work with you just because you spoke up for yourself. After all, the majority rules.

Make sure your finances are somewhat in order before you make a formal complaint. When you first go, you will need to contact your attorney and go through the protocol. You have to go to HR, but once you do, the cat is out of the bag. They are going to let the bad apple know what you reported. They are going to let your boss, CEO, and CFO know what is happening. All of the guys and girls are going to know what you have reported. Once that happens, there is a high chance you are not going to want to sit at that desk every day because now it is intense. You might have the intimidation factor coming. You are going to get thrown more work with no invite to informal meetings. It is going to be a lot on your back. You will feel the heat because people are now after you. They are looking at you like a tattle-tale. Make sure your finances are in check because once you take action, your attorney may say you should go to your primary doctor and let them know you are stressed so you can get a week or two off of work. Make sure you are in somewhat of a place to skip a paycheck or two. I know this might be hard for the every-day working person because most of us do live check-to-check. You have to choose your health, most importantly your mental health, over any company or any role.

The Real Truth

Melody

When it came time to pull the wool from their eyes, most of the bosses and administrators acted shocked that I was bringing racist accusations about them to the table. If I am saying I believe a situation is racist, I am basically labeling others as racist people. No one wants to be called a racist even if they are and I have all the apples and oranges to prove it. It immediately shifted to a hostile work environment. If I eventually did not walk away from the job, they would push me out. That happened on a couple of occasions. Either they were adding more to my workload and it was becoming overwhelming, or I was being left out of meetings and important conversations or being shunned on the job. It weighed heavily on me mentally, physically, spiritually, and financially as well because I was not getting the promotion or the raises.

Usually when you call that bad apple out, HR wants to know witnesses–individuals who were involved and can attest to the situations happening. Usually, they approach people in your department. No one wants to be pulled into that because they question what it will mean to tell the truth. Will they experience some repercussions? Retaliation? Or lose their job trying to stick up for you when it is not their situation? I had a boss who was very aware of my supervisor and my senior manager when I was experiencing racism in the hostile work environment. She knew what was going on. We talked about it in our one-on-one. We had a mediation with the employee's attorney, and my boss was subpoenaed to speak about the situation. They asked her if I had ever come to her and mentioned that I thought this was a racist situation. It took her a long time to answer.

She kept her head down and said, *"No, she never told me."*

I was very disappointed because I did tell her on several occasions what was happening to me and not happening to "Suzy Jane." At the end of the day, I feel like this is a racist tactic. I told her that on several occasions.

When we got in front of legal, she said *"No"* and carried on.

It was my word against hers, and I had not documented or written down anywhere that I felt I was working in a racist environment. It was on her to do what was right, which was to tell the truth, and she did not.

Monica

There is a one-in-a-million chance you get that one coworker who just might support you in your reporting to HR. I had it one time out of my 15-plus-year career. I worked with her, and she was a project manager. One white lady noticed the racist, sexist treatment. She knew what was happening, and she said she was going to HR. That was the one time out of so many different situations I had reported that I had support. So many colleagues and so-called friends turned their backs on me. It is rare that you get that one employee who knows what is right is right and what is wrong is wrong.

The next thing you have to be prepared for is the backlash of not being able to put the company on your resume as a reference. If you report someone, it would not be a good idea to put them or the firm on your resume. They are upset you reported them, so what do you think they are going to tell a new potential employer about you? You have to strategically think about how you are going to write out your resume. I have experience and do not want to leave too many jobs off of my resume that will then not reveal my accomplishments. Make sure you have standing relationships and former coworkers you can count on to support you when you need references. Future employers do want to complete a background check on you to determine what you are like, what you have done, where you have worked, and who you know.

LET'S EXAMINE

ANALYZING GENDER AND RACE IN THE WORKPLACE

1. The Past vs. The Present: Understanding The Equal Pay Act of 1963

In 2021, 49% of Latinos and 51% of Black women had trouble paying for their food, housing, or childcare.

"How the System Is Failing Latinas and Black Women." *Lean In*, 2021, leanin.org.

The earnings of females were less than two-thirds of those of males by 1960. In the United States, the Equal Pay Act prohibits gender-based wage discrimination. According to the law, equal pay for equal work is required as part of the Fair Labor Standards Act, which was signed by President John F. Kennedy in 1963. Under the act, employers cannot pay women or men differently for jobs requiring the same skills and responsibilities. It was one of the first laws to address workplace discrimination in American history. Gender-based wage discrimination, which dates back centuries, was addressed by the Equal Pay Act. Women made up a quarter of the workforce but were paid less than men even when doing the same job ("Equal Pay Act"). It was praised by President Kennedy as a "significant step forward," even as he acknowledged that "much more needs to be done" to fully equalize women's economic opportunity. Kennedy was also an advocate for having daycare facilities to support working women. A discrimination complaint can be filed with the Equal Employment Opportunity Commission, or employees can sue their employers directly if they feel they have been discriminated against. The combination of regulations, educational opportunities, and career advancements put forth in the act has been credited with helping to narrow the gender wage gap. Even so, studies indicate that women continue to earn less than men. In 2020, full-time women workers earned 83 cents for every dollar earned by full-time men, according to estimates from the Bureau of Labor Statistics (Iacurci).

LeanIn.Org and SurveyMonkey reported in 2021 that paying for necessities like childcare and rent is difficult for half of Latinas and Black women. This is magnified by the finding that half of these women also have less than $300 in emergency savings ("How the System"). Though financial issues increased for many families during and post-pandemic, Covid-19 was not the catalyst for this economic inequity that began long before the pandemic. A Latina or Black woman, on average, receives a lower wage than white men and women. The number of low-wage jobs they hold exceeds their proportion in the labor force. Paid leave and other benefits are less available to them. There is also a greater likelihood they will not be approved for a home loan. These systemic problems have existed for a long time, and they require systemic solutions. Pay gaps between whites and Blacks must be closed by business leaders. There must be policies put into place that directly address the issues that impact Black and Latina women disproportionately. LeanIn. org's article suggests implementing policies like minimum wage increases to at least $15 an hour, improvements to childcare access and implementation where it does not exist, and putting in place a national paid family leave policy ("How the System").

Many other laws were passed to reduce employment discrimination following the passage of the Equal Pay Act. In Title VII of the Civil Rights Act of 1964, ethnic, racial, religious, sexist, and national origin discrimination is prohibited ("Know Your Rights"). Under this law, sex and race discrimination is prohibited in hiring, promoting, and terminating employees. Also, federally funded programs are prohibited from discrimination. In addition, voting rights were strengthened and school segregation improved. In the state and federal arenas and in every industry of all sizes, the non-profit organization Equal Rights Advocates has been fighting for equal pay for more than 45 years. Legal, policy, and cultural barriers have been responsible for persisting gender wage gaps for many years. Equal Rights Advocates challenges these barriers and will continue to do so until true change is made.

2. Demystifying Equality

A UN study found that 90% of both women
and men hold prejudice toward women.

Gilchrist, Karen. "Men Are Not the Only Ones
Biased against Women, UN Study Finds." *CNBC*,
CNBC, 6 Mar. 2020, www.cnbc.com.

To understand the progress that has been made and obstacles that remain to achieve gender equality, it is necessary to consider whether the status and role of women have changed over the years. According to the Pew Research Center, in a survey aiming to identify what words Americans identify with each gender, words like 'multitasking,' 'stylish,' and 'maternal' have exclusively been used for women (Bialik). These findings reveal the degree to which gender biases and characterizations are rooted in our society. In the Pew Research survey, 51% of people feel that women should be independent, while 49% feel otherwise (Bialik). Women are traditionally expected to fill submissive roles in a society that views men as more dominant. The subversion of sexism and traditional gender norms is an unexpected reality. When brilliance, genius, and innate intelligence are perceived as masculine attributes, then women are left out of disciplines that demand such qualities. Bias against women is, in essence, a double-edged sword. In other words, we either demonstrate qualities that make us too soft to be good leaders or show more masculine characteristics that make us appear too aggressive to be a good leader. Men and women are both affected by masculine/feminine stereotypes.

Views such as these group people into certain boxes. When individuals demonstrate qualities that are different from the norm, they are more likely to be viewed unequally. As a result, these biases become embedded in work-place culture. Dismantling them through active engagement and awareness will enable us to move forward with the goal of true equality. More than a century ago, the U.S. legislature passed the 19th Amendment, stipulating that women would be allowed to vote. Disenfranchisement, both then and now, has been recognized as a blight on the nation and a hindrance to the U.S.'s ability to become a functioning democracy through hard-fought efforts of women and men. Despite the 19th Amendment's promise to provide voting rights for women regardless of race, Black women faced difficulty in practicing that right in the face of the Jim Crow era (Jones). Black women's right to vote was truly secured in 1965 with the Voting Rights Act, passed nearly half a century after the 19th Amendment, underscoring the fact that race and gender have always been important factors for women of color (Jones).

Racial and gender disparities continue to exist for women of all races and especially for Black women. Women employed in professional occupations are especially underrepresented and experience these issues. The racial and gender divides in the workplace continue to disadvantage Black women. Researchers have found that both factors negatively impact women across a variety of occupations as they experience decreased leadership opportunities; sexual harassment; and doubts about their competence, intelligence, and skills. Also, Black women are less likely to find mentors who will aid their climb up the corporate ladder. Lack of mentoring is a result of intentionally excluding Black women from teams, mentee roles, and important projects. Black women are hindered by these patterns in reaching their goals and achieving leadership positions. Black women also face discrimination and underrepresentation in leadership roles, which results in wage disparities and occupational underrepresentation.

3. Equal Pay vs. Equal Value

At the current rate of progress, no equal pay until 2069.

"Equal Pay for Work of Equal Value." *UN Women*, 2017, www.unwomen.org.

Not only in the United States but across the world, women are paid less than their male counterparts. There are several considerations to address in the discussion of leveling the playing ground for women. The question that we must ask ourselves is whether or not we live in a society that values the work of women equally to our male counterparts. Furthermore, what can be done to lessen the gap and who will be responsible for this work?

According to a report on closing the gender pay gap by UN Women in 2016, because of traditional gender roles and discrimination, closing the gender pay gap is an ever-evolving problem. Women are overrepresented in fields that are designated as traditionally "women's work." When women enter the workforce in male-dominated fields, gender discrimination can intensify or morph into new lines. Even worse is that gender pay gap laws can often be insufficient in stopping pay discrimination. These laws restrict women to identifying unfair pay only amongst men who work similar jobs within the same establishment which, according to UN Women, "ignores the reality of widespread labor market segregation on the basis of gender (Tackling)."

With insufficient legal protection comes demand for workplaces to take it upon themselves to ensure equal pay. This would require organizations to be transparent with their wages, an act that is often seen as taboo in the workplace.

4. Dissecting The Gender Pay Gap

"This widening of the gap goes hand in hand with trends recorded in a report issued by the World Economic Forum which found that gender parity has shifted in reverse for the first time since 2006."

Qureshi, Lyla. "Dissecting C-Suite Gender Pay Disparity." *The Harvard Law School Forum on Corporate Governance*, 1 Aug. 2018, corpgov.law.harvard.edu.

There can be many issues when it comes to dissecting and analyzing the gender pay gap. Equilar, a company that focuses on data-driven solutions for businesses, took a look at the gender pay equity ratio in 2018 while examining specifically those at the executive level. They did so initially by calculating the total compensation of both male and female CEOs. While examining the pay, Equilar found that in 2015, the average female CEO earned 1% less than their male counterparts. In 2016, the women studied actually earned 3% more than the men with an increasing trend toward 2018 (Qureshi). The issue with this data is that the sample pool for women in those positions is rather small. When the data was measured in 2017, there were just 135 female CEOs. Then they expanded to measure general counsel at Russell 3000 market index companies, CEOs, CFOs, and HR executives (Qureshi).

When examining CFOs between the years of 2015 and 2017, Equilar found that men consistently made more than their female counterparts. In fact, they made 11.2% more (Qureshi). During that same period, female executives serving as general counsel saw a 4.3% difference in 2016 which then expanded to 7% in 2017 (Qureshi). HR executives experienced the greatest pay ratio when compared to men with the wage gap rising 28.1% between 2015 and 2017 (Qureshi).

This data is consistent with the findings of the 2017 Global Gender Gap Report, which showed that for the first time since 2006, the gender gap was actually reversing rather than closing (Qureshi). The Harvard Law School Forum discussed these findings with Anna Beninger, senior director of Research at Catalyst, who stated, "Few women make it to those jobs where they're making hundreds of millions of dollars, so they're really seen as the exception rather than the rule, and so that impacts their ability to negotiate. Moreover, when women do tend to negotiate, they are treated differently than men" (Qureshi). When women do negotiate for promotions or better pay, they are often seen as "aggressive" which can lead to "negative results" (Qureshi).

5. Gender Wage Gap or Gender Earnings Gap?

"Much of the gender earnings gap is explained
by gender differences in labor force attachment
and accumulated labor market experience."

Canon, Maria E., et al. "Understanding the Gender
Earnings Gap: Hours Worked, Occupational Sorting, and
Labor Market Experience." *Economic Research - Federal
Reserve Bank of St. Louis*, 2021, research.stlouisfed.org.

Some propose that the gender pay gap doesn't exist at all, rather it is a gender earnings gap that does. Mark J. Perry, an American economist and professor of economics and finance in the School of Management at the University of Michigan–Flint, states that the issue of combatting the earnings gap must be addressed first at the level of vocabulary used to describe and identify the issue.

Perry states that "It's an important but overlooked point that there really is no gender wage gap, rather, there's a gender earnings gap and that pay gap has almost nothing to do with gender discrimination (Perry)."

According to Perry, the issue presented is not that women and men are paid differently for the same jobs, rather women tend to be oversaturated in lower-wage jobs and men tend to be oversaturated in higher-paying jobs, like sciences and manual labor. In order for the gender wage gap to be closed from this standpoint, many other gender gaps that "do exist" would need to be closed (Perry). Perry suggests that the reason women are not represented within these environments comes primarily from their own choice, among other issues.

An article by Maria E. Canon and other economists for the Economic Research Federal Reserve Bank of St. Louis states that occupations tend to reward those who work long hours and punish those who take off or choose to work fewer hours (Canon). This system especially punishes women in "childbearing" years, as well as impacts what choices they have for occupations.

Canon posits that as the gap in weekly hours grows, so does the gap in wages. Also proposed is that the fewer hours an employee works, the less experience they are considered to have, something Perry also proposes (Canon). According to Perry, there are more men who have extensive and continuous work experience than women, which partially accounts for the earnings gap (Perry).

Though the distinction between the "gender pay gap" and the "earnings gap" can lead to effective discourse and studies on the issue, there is often a lack of consideration of social issues such as gender and discrimination in the workplace as discussed in section 4. Women are not taught the skills needed to negotiate for pay increases and promotions, which would reduce the "gender earnings gap." Even when those skills are taught, it is not always socially acceptable for women to utilize them (Qureshi).

Ruth Thomas, a pay equity strategist at Payscale, is noted as stating, "One of the arguments we often hear is that the pay gap exists because of women's career choices, but I would question whether those are actual choices, or choices forced on women, who are often limited to certain sectors because of a lack of paid family leave and flexibility in others (Smith)."

The pay gap is more complex and legitimate than Perry and others who argue against it recognize.

6. Gender Pay Gap Examples

When we talk about workplace equity, we're talking about far more than equal pay – it's also about creating environments where everyone feels supported and has access to the same opportunities."

Smith, Morgan. "These 5 Industries Have the Biggest Gender Pay Gaps-Here's Why." *CNBC*, 30 Mar. 2022, www.cnbc.com.

There are many examples that exist throughout the workforce of the gender pay gap. In fact, experts suspect that the wage gap will increase in certain industries due to the economic turmoil resulting from the 2020 pandemic. Industries with the largest gender pay gaps include finance, consultancies, health care, transportation/warehousing, and nonprofits. What makes these pay gaps so surprising is that as of 2022, women make up around 76% of health care workers within the United States as well as 65% of nonprofit workers (Smith).

An article by Morgan Smith for CNBC shows that even when women pursue advanced degrees that are often required for higher payer jobs, the pay gap can have the reverse effect and widen rather than close. Payscale's 2022 State of Gender Pay Gap Report found that for women with MBAs, the uncontrolled pay gap is 76 cents for every dollar a man with an MBA makes (Smith). For women with law degrees, that uncontrolled pay gap is 89 cents when compared to their male counterparts (Smith).

In their controlled studies, Payscale found that the gap was closer than the uncontrolled. However, even if the controlled pay gap was closed, the uncontrolled pay gap would continue to persist since high-paying jobs are continued to be more easily accessible to men than women (Smith).

The industries that have the smallest uncontrolled pay gap unsurprisingly have more women in senior positions. Those industries, including arts, real estate, construction, and education, often offer more "flexible work arrangements" that aid women who take on traditional caregiving responsibilities.

7. Gender Pay Gap and The Pandemic

"Women earn less because they are more likely to leave the workforce as a result of social expectations placed on them as mothers and caretakers, heightened by the pandemic."

Miller, Stephen. "Gender Pay Gap Improvement Slowed During the Pandemic." *SHRM*, SHRM, 15 Mar. 2022, www.shrm.org.

The "uncontrolled" pay gap from 2021 to 2022 remains unchanged with women earning 82 cents per every dollar a man makes (Miller). This lack of change marks stagnation from the continuous improvement seen in earlier years. Other sources suggest that the pay gap continued to rise into 2022 (Miller). However, understanding this statistic has become more complex with the pandemic. Women left the workforce in greater numbers than men, especially women with high school education levels or lower. From the end of 2019 to the end of 2021, women with no high school degree in the workforce decreased by 12.8% (Fry). This is a significantly larger number than their male counterparts whose saturation in the workplace decreased by 4.9% (Fry). For women with a high school diploma, their presence in the workforce decreased by 6% compared to similarly educated men whose employment level fell by 1.8% (Fry).

The withdrawal of less-educated women with a high school diploma reflects women being overrepresented in industries such as food preparation, personal service occupations, and health care (Fry). This is also reflective of women being overrepresented in industries requiring them to work on-site, which became incredibly difficult during the pandemic. The pay gap also tremendously impacted Black and brown women of color in the workplace throughout the pandemic (Miller).

Following the pandemic, employers are seeing more employers working to create equitable environments and pay for their employees. According to an article on SHRM by Stephen Miller, workplaces are finally thinking beyond gender and putting the focus on every "unexplained" pay gap. This includes pay gaps for Black and brown women.

Ruth Thomas, a pay equity strategist at Payscale, suggests, "As salary structures are adjusted in response to rising wage inflation, minimum wage increases and strong competition for talent, employers should 'continuously monitor pay equity.'"

Caveats

Melody

Black women are highly ambitious and assertive, which are skills needed to be an effective leader. Similar traits are also displayed by white men, and that is one of the reasons that you see them as your CEOs, executives, CFOs, and in other leadership positions. White men are praised for having this type of leadership style, and unfortunately it is the opposite for Black women. Black women don't excel in the same roles as white men. However studies show we are very similiar in our leadership styles. It is almost like we are reprimanded for having the same skills that white men are rewarded for having. When it comes to our counterparts, white male leaders, they really need to learn how to ally with and advocate for Black women in the workplace. Speaking up for us when things are not right on our behalf because most of the time we are the only women and/or Black woman in the room. We don't have the same privilege. When people say that they want to be an ally to Black women, that means being accountable and standing up when we are facing racism or sexual harassment.

In the past couple of years, I had one person who stood up for me. It was a situation where I went to advocate for more pay in a consulting role. I had a previous conversation with the leader in regard to getting a raise that we started and decided to re-evaluate at the end of the month. The leader was an Asian woman and when I went back to speak to her, she began to become very hostile. The conversation became very intense and she proceeded to tell me that the pay that I was asking for was more than what she was paying her CEOs which later resulted in her repeating my current pay rate as if I should be satisfied and had no room to be negotiating for more. Remind you we had already discussed having this follow up conversation about increase in pay early on when I agreed to take on the role. We know that most CEOs are white males, so what she basically said was that what I was coming to the table and bargaining for was more than what she was even paying her white males. I told her that it was fine but proceeded to tell her why I felt that I deserved the pay that I was negotiating and what I had been doing on the job.

The conversation didn't end on good terms. That was the first time that I spoke up for myself and told her that the way she was having the conversation was very unprofessional. I told her that if I were a white male, she never would have said that, and if I was a woman of another race, she would not have said that to me. It was a subtle microaggression stemming from the thought it was absurd that I, as a Black woman, was coming and asking for the pay that I was seeking, even though the rate that I was asking for wasn't unheard of.

What happened afterward was that I told the person who I was actually working for on behalf of the company that I was going to be ending the role with the client. I didn't feel that the leader was advocating for me with the client. That conversation just didn't feel right and the client must have heard that I was going to be ending the role because he called me. He was an Indian male and the director of his department. He asked me what had happened, and I explained the story to him.

He said, "*Listen, you are doing great in the role. What do we need to do to keep you here? Whatever you need, the pay you are asking for, don't worry about it. I will work with her to get it.*"

That was the first time someone, especially a male of another race, had advocated for me, and I got the pay I was asking for. I ended up staying in that role for another year because of the relationship I was able to build with that leader who spoke up for me. While I am thankful for this person standing up on my behalf, I am also aware that this doesn't happen often for Black women. In most situations like this we are left trying to solve the issue on our own which can be difficult.

Monica

When you are talking about racism, similar to sexual abuse or sexual harassment on the job, it is a different form but it is all considered harassment. Black women are the most unprotected and disrespected inside and outside of the workplace. So when you do get into the professional setting, nobody feels that they have to speak up on your behalf. If there is something uncomfortable going on, no one will come to your aid, whereas, if white or Asian women even drop a tear, everyone rallies around them. They might even get the CFO or the VP involved and people rally around that particular woman. When it's a Black woman, you don't see that.

In my 16 years of professional experience, I have only had one woman stand up for me. She noticed the harassment I was facing from the CFO of the company I was working at and stood by me. There needs to be more.

Commentary

Monica

People in the workplace need to believe and trust in Black women. When we say things, when we speak up, when we share advice or an opinion. Trust and believe in Black women. Allow Black women to be soft. Allow Black women to take breaks and not force us to be superhuman doing so many things and going a mile a minute. Allow us some grace similar to what you do for other women.

Melody

Black women deserve to be valued and respected in the workplace. Historically, people have viewed Black women as less than or less deserving than our white and other counterparts. Our contributions bring so much value to the workplace. We need, want, and deserve respect.

Yes, I understand the "Black girl magic" motivation, but Black women must also be recognized as human. There's this notion that we can do anything and go through anything as if we are superhuman. We wear this invisible courage like armor, but at times we do feel broken, discouraged, unseen and unheard. We do have feelings. We are human, and we are not supernatural.

CASE STUDY

SHANNON POWER, VP OF FINANCE

1.   WHAT WAS YOUR FIRST EXPERIENCE WITH SEXISM IN THE WORKPLACE?

The first one I can legally talk about occurred very early on in my career. I was working for a large corporation at the time. They needed a project manager ,and I was the engineer who was chosen for the role. At the time, I was traveling for work and happened to be near the project sponsor's location, so I decided to go and introduce myself to him. I met him and the very next day, I found out from my manager that I had been removed from the project. They had given the project manager role to one of my male colleagues. I was confused and spoke with my management team about it.

I asked for an explanation as to why I was removed from the project and they replied, *"Well, you'd be too much of a distraction so we're going to move you to something else."*

My jaw fell to the floor. I couldn't believe what they had said to me. The work was taken from me, given to someone else, and I was reassigned to another project. Nothing was done. My manager felt that the project sponsor was justified in wanting to choose whatever project manager he wanted. Early on in my career, I didn't know what I was supposed to do. Being a female engineer, especially and unfortunately, I was used to being discriminated against because I was a female. Even in college, I was once accused of cheating because my lab professor couldn't believe that I was intelligent enough to complete an assignment. By my early career, I was so used to it that I thought that was just how it was.

2. HOW DID THE DISCRIMINATION IMPACT YOUR CAREER GOING FORWARD?

The discrimination made me work harder because I wanted to get to a point where I felt that *I* was the decision maker where I didn't feel like I had these decisions being chosen for me. It motivated me to work as hard as I possibly could so I could move up. I wanted to have control over my project choices and my career path going forward.

3. DID YOU GET ANY SUPPORT FROM YOUR MANAGER OR COLLEAGUES AFTER FACING THIS DISCRIMINATION?

Yes and no. Some colleagues were extremely supportive.

One of the reasons that I didn't dwell on this experience was because colleagues would tell me, *"You didn't want that one anyway. Let me introduce you to someone else who you would work well with."*

My colleagues took the extra step to try and help me network within the organization. They advocated for me, and I felt supported. They were personally taking the time to ask their managers for one-on-one meetings with me, especially if they knew that they had a manager who was open to diverse teams.

4. NOW THAT YOU ARE A VP LEVEL, DO YOU FEEL THAT CEOS CARE ABOUT FEMALE ISSUES IN THE WORKPLACE?

Some do, but some I'm not certain. In late 2022, I was contacted by multiple recruiters looking to hire their next CFO. They were specifically looking for a female with hopes of hiring a woman of color. They were intentionally seeking diversity on their team, and I give kudos to those CEOs who are doing so. There have been enough studies that show that diverse teams lead to an increase in profitability. Why are there so many CEOs who still ignore this?

Other CEOs, I'm not so sure. What I look for to tell if CEOs are truly caring about women in the workplace is if they have female advisors and executive teams, not just HR. Do these companies have advisors in areas that are traditionally lower in percentages of females? You can look at the executive teams of all public and most private companies.

5. CAN YOU TELL ME ABOUT THE FIRST EXPERIENCE WHERE YOU WITNESSED RACISM IN THE WORKPLACE?

Very early on in my career I was working for a company that, like many companies, had their entry-level employees in an open office area. It was very easy to hear dialogue throughout the office. I was in an environment with all men and one day I could hear some of them talking and sharing jokes about Asian people. We had several Asian people sitting near us. I heard the first joke and was sitting uncomfortably in my seat listening to them. I wanted to get up and say something, but I was worried that I would also be targeted. By the third joke, I had had enough.

I stood up and said, *"Y'all can't do this here. This is not appropriate."*

They all looked at me as if they couldn't understand why I had spoken. They said, *"What? Is your boyfriend Asian?"*

I replied, *"It doesn't matter. This is not the appropriate place to say this."*

They laughed at me and said, *"Ok, HR."*

I went back to my desk and continued working. They stopped, but I received a cold shoulder from those men from then on. There was no HR involvement and no other coworker spoke up.

CASE STUDY

KIM CRAYTON, ANTIRACIST ECONOMIST

1. WHAT WAS YOUR FIRST EXPERIENCE WITH RACISM IN THE WORKPLACE?

Honestly, I don't remember my first experience with racism. I've always experienced it, but I wasn't always aware of it. It's interesting because I grew up in the South, so of course I knew what white supremacy was and I knew about racism, but we did not use the language. So, as a Black woman who was indeed having these experiences with racism and prejudice and racial bias, I could not pinpoint or accurately express what was happening to me because I did not have the language. One experience that comes to mind is when I was working on my undergraduate degree. I was an interior design major and at the time I had a really good friend, a white friend. I observed as she advanced in ways that I knew were not right. I watched as my white friend, who did not have the experience I had and who did not work as hard as I did, advanced in ways I know I should have. The unfortunate thing is, this insidious behavior is really quiet. There was another time when I was still an undergraduate and I worked at the Chicago Board of Trade. I started in my late 20s and I was on the floor with the traders. As a trader, we were responsible for putting what was being traded in the machine and keeping the data of the supply. The majority of traders were arrogant, wealthy white men who treated the small number of Black people like they did not belong. Ironically, even in that moment, I still did not have the language to pinpoint what was so obvious and what I knew did not feel right. I knew I was being discriminated against. I knew they were being racist, but I still did not have the language.

2. WHEN WERE YOU ABLE TO DEVELOP THE LANGUAGE TO SPEAK ON YOUR EXPERIENCES WITH RACISM?

It was just eight years ago when I entered tech. One day I witnessed a white dude who was a keynote speaker, and he stood and talked about his privilege. I was floored. That was when I went down this rabbit hole and started listening to people. Again, as a Black woman I have that lived experience, but it took me to actually hear a white dude say, *"I have these privileges and these privileges afford me things you do not have."* This began my own journey of unpacking and researching these systems such as the police. I learned that the reason there is a higher number of Black people who are incarcerated or getting killed by the police is because policing started in slavery with the injustice of catching slaves. Once I started unpacking this, I began seeing it everywhere. As Black people, we spend our lives trying to protect ourselves from something we cannot see, we cannot touch, we don't understand until a white person calls it out and a light bulb goes off. Now, that isn't the case for everybody. I understand that there are some who experienced this revelation earlier than I did. Though I have been in spaces that were full of Black Power, no one talked about it like this to me. It took a white man who lives this life to say, to admit, that the game was rigged. He started on home base and as Black people, we are not even on the field. We are in the parking lot.

3. NOW THAT YOU HAVE BEEN DOWN THE RABBIT HOLE, TELL ME ABOUT WHEN YOU STARTED TAKING THE STEPS TO CALL OUT RACISM.

Since forever, when people talk about tech they think Google and the Internet but that is simply information. That did not lead me to knowledge, so I decided to go back to school. In 2014, I started my doctoral program. I was determined to learn how to build businesses. It wasn't until I started getting my first clients that I really began to see what I had always lived through.

Let me do a caveat. When I witnessed that white guy say what he said, it was because tech at that point was starting to realize how much harm they were causing with the products and services they were making on a global scale. Tech was reckoning with what other industries had never had to reckon with because they could hide it. However, it got to the point where the tech industry realized that what they were making was racist. This is why it became the conversation in tech. When I started getting my first clients who understood about their privileges, that is when the advocacy really began to unravel.

I started to realize these people did not have businesses. What they had was a product of services they've been able to scale, and we're seeing that now with this "recession." We're seeing that when when you don't have investors throwing money at you just to scale your business, you really don't have a business. You've had the benefit of money to be able to acquire customers and users, but you don't have a business. Those organization's leaders understood this and so I I couldn't do my business because I'm a business strategist. I could not do business strategy because no one was dealing with and talking about the white supremacy that was inherent in these companies. This is why diversity, equity and inclusion efforts, also known as DEI, are failing. People often say I am a DEI specialist but no, I am not a DEI specialist. I make it my business to talk about DEI because I can't get to the business aspect because there isn't anything there. In this economy we're not making widgets anymore and so how organizational leaders profit, innovate, differentiate, and compete with other places is that they need the knowledge out of my head, which they hired me for. These companies hire me for my lived experience. They're not hiring me to make widgets where a manual is given and I make my widget look like everybody else's. They hire me for my lived experience and my expertise derived from my lived experience. However, if I do not feel safe inside your organization, if every day is a battle and every day I am subjected to professional violence because I don't call it microaggression, if I am being subjected to professional violence in small and large ways, that information in my head is going to stay in my head. So it does not benefit the organization. It was finally between 2016-2018 when I just said "Fuck it! I'm going to talk about this." That is when I started causing a scene and did not hold anything back. At that point. I was not making any money. Everyone wanted me to talk but no one wanted to hire me. They wanted me to talk for free, but white men aren't being asked to talk for free. I decided that I didn't have anything else to lose, so I'm just going to stir up a whole bunch of shit.

4. CAN YOU TALK ABOUT THE WAGE DISCRIMINATION THAT YOU HAVE EXPERIENCED?

If I am being hired for my lived experience and I am valued as a person for the specific thing, why am I not being hired? If the corporate owners see my lived experience as significant to their company and I am valued as a person who has my lived experience, why is my expertise considered free? Even if I was a DEI expert, why do you think that this vital work that is going to help you differentiate, innovate and be competitive, should be discounted? Why is it not a problem for these corporate owners to ask me to speak about mentoring or whatever my lived experience is that can benefit their business and boldly expect it to be free. It is automatically assumed the service will be free. I am in a place now where even getting a cup of coffee is going to cost you. White people and white supremacy changed my whole way of operating. If you want to meet me for coffee, it will cost you $600. I don't do anything for free because of how I now understand things. For example, information asymmetry. As Black people and Black women, we come from community, but whiteness is not about community. We understand that one must give to receive, but that is not how this operates and as a result, we just give and give and give and get nothing in return. White supremacy is not a reciprocal relationship at all. I learned and understood this, and that is when I began to change how I operated.

I was being called to speak at different engagements and being flown around the world but when I looked in my bank account, I had nothing. I was being told how great I was and how I am changing their business. I am changing your business, but I can't eat! The crazy part is they don't even think about it. Corporate owners are flying people out and Black women are getting free tickets to conferences but they need a card for their file. Why are you allowing the hotel to hold these people's card information if you're paying for everything? I've been to these conferences where the hotel would not let me check in without using my card information, which means they will put a hold on my account for money that I thought I was going to eat with. It all turns into a whole absolute shitshow because people don't consider the situations they are creating that are perpetuating racism or perpetuating me to be victimized and harmed.

5. NOW THAT YOU ARE IN THE SPACE TO BE YOUR OWN ADVOCATE, DO YOU HAVE ANY WHITE COUNTERPARTS WHO SUPPORTED YOUR PLATFORM?

I would not have gotten this far without white people because the ones who got it were the ones who would say *"Kim, you need to charge"* because I wasn't charging. They were the ones telling me that my prices were too low, again information asymmetry. I'm not supposed to know this information. Unless they told me I was at a disadvantage. This is why I have a problem when people talk about equality. It isn't about equality, it's about equity because as a Black woman, I was never seen as your equal. When we discuss equality or equal payday, to me it is a bunch of bullshit. I need you to not only get me to where my counterparts are but you need to give me my back salary and that does not account for all the things I missed out on, the things I could not afford because you were not paying me. These are the things people do not want to talk about. They do not want to talk about reparation because it's not just about giving me a check, especially with how current systems, institutions, and policies are designed. This is why I challenge Black people to talk about more than getting a check. Just receiving a check is a set-up. As soon as they give you their check, that money is going to go back into their pockets, trust me. You will not have that money for long. We have enough data on how lottery winners are broke in 10 years and not only broke, but in further debt. This is what will happen if we only receive a check through reparations. White supremacy exploits and once they give us that money, the systems, institutions and policies in place will cause that money to go right back. Once the money goes back, the narrative will be that the money was wasted. The narrative will be *"You gave these Black people this money and they wasted this money."* This understanding and how I built my company came from white people saying *"Kim, you need to get paid. Kim, your fees aren't high enough. Kim, are you resting?"* With the community I have, I know I'm very unique. I have a group of volunteers who build my websites and who deal with my 80 graphics. I do not pay white people. They volunteer their services to me. My actual company consists of myself and a part-time assistant. The support I have is from white people who want to see me succeed, who understand what I have to say is important and they want to make sure the word gets out. At times people get confused and believe I hate white people but I don't. I just know how to put them in their place. I need to teach them there's a lane for you to help and there's a lane for you to shut up. I need for you to know this because this is not about you.

6. WHEN YOU LOOK AT BIG COMPANIES, DO YOU FEEL THAT THEY CARE ABOUT BLACK OR FEMALE ISSUES IN THE WORKPLACE?

That's the wrong question to ask because it doesn't matter how they feel. That's why white supremacy and anti-blackness works so well. They don't have to do anything to be racist for them to benefit from it, so they can feel any way they want to. However, the systems, institutions, and policies designed are always going to benefit them, and not just benefit them but benefit them at my expense. That is what people do not understand. It is not just that white people are privileged. That is only part of the equation. The other part is they are privileged and their privilege comes at my expense. It comes as a direct result of me being harmed. So let's not get into these corner conversations that distract us. I do not get into those conversations because I know it is nonbinary. They are privileged and I am harmed. It is not that they are privileged and it doesn't impact me. No. Their privilege impacts me. This is why intention without strategy is chaos. White people can have the best intentions but if you do not have a strategy for countering the inherent bias and racism that's already in the systems, institutions, and policies, nothing changes. Again, this is why DEI doesn't work. Let's give an example. If they have a stack that is $1,000 and they say *"Kim I want to give you an equal stack,"* your giving me a stack of $1,000 does not work for me. Why? Because my $1,000 and your $1,000 do not buy the same things. That is the conversation we need to have. Your $1,000 does not have the barriers my $1,000 has. If we both take that $1,000 to put a down payment on a house, because you have better rates and less barriers, your $1,000 will get you more house than my $1,000 is going to get me. This is the conversation we need to have.

7. WHAT IS YOUR VIEW WHEN IT COMES TO THE EQUAL PAY MOVEMENT?

I don't even want to talk about equal pay until we talk about equity. We can never get to equal pay until we talk about equity. We are not and never were equal. Equal pay is a lie or misnomer thatagain presumes you give me a dollar and it matches your dollar. . It does not. Until we talk about equity, we can never get to equal because let's be honest, I was never meant to be equal to you. I should still be a slave. They never considered us in any of these things except to be of service to them. Until you see me as someone who's not of service to you, we cannot talk about equality. That is why they get so mad when Black women center themselves because the only value we have in this society that they deem us for is to take care of other people, not ourselves.

One of the things that I talk about when it comes to starting a new company is how to change the narrative. Given that systems, institutions, and policies are designed to privilege white people and harm people of color, Black people specifically, take out everything else and talk about pay. You as an organizational leader make the decision, no one in my organization makes less than that set number. It does not matter if they're the CEO or they're cleaning the toilets. No one makes less than this because this is a living wage in my community.

8. WHAT ARE YOUR CLOSING STATEMENTS ON WHAT YOU WANT BLACK WOMEN TO LEARN OR UNDERSTAND ABOUT THE POWER THEY HAVE IN ANY FIELD THEY ARE IN?

Black women are the moral compass and our collective liberation is through us. You go to any community around the world and you find the darkest person is the person who has the answers to the suffering because they've been inflicted. They've been the target. I want Black women to know that they should do away with imposter syndrome. Imposter syndrome is defined as a person who's an expert in something but still lacks confidence in their abilities. Right there are two parts of that. They are erroneous in that and how people use it. First of all, a lot of Black people and a lot of people who are new to something use imposter syndrome because they're struggling, but you're not struggling. You do not know anything yet, you are learning. You are not an expert. How can you have imposter syndrome when you have yet to become an expert in that category? Stop saying that you are suffering from imposter syndrome. You don't know anything yet. You are learning. The second one is imposter syndrome is rooted in white supremacy and anti-Blackness because it doesn't account for the systems, institutions, and policies that are designed to make us fail and not succeed. We then internalize it and say to ourselves, "*We must be missing something*" when we are not.

Lastly, as a Black woman, you must learn to take up space, both physically and metaphorically. Take up space. I tell white people, I want you to pay attention to how you walk around the mall and how you walk around on the sidewalk expecting people to get out of your way. I don't do that anymore. We will come head to head. I will brace myself to knock your shit over. I do not care if you're in a stroller or walker, get the hell out my way. So, Black women learn to take up space both physically and metaphorically.

Let's Discuss

1. Do you believe sexism/racism exists in your workplace
    and have you personally experienced it?

_____

_____

_____

_____

_____

_____

_____

_____

_____

_____

_____

_____

Let's Discuss

2. Is HR a helpful resource?

_____

_____

_____

_____

_____

_____

_____

_____

_____

_____

_____

_____

Let's Discuss

3. Is the pay gap real?

_____

_____

_____

_____

_____

_____

_____

_____

_____

_____

_____

_____

_____

Let's Discuss

4. Do CEOs care about female issues in the workplace?

_____

_____

_____

_____

_____

_____

_____

_____

_____

_____

_____

_____

Let's Discuss

5. Did you know about the Equal Pay Act of 1963 before today?

_____

_____

_____

_____

_____

_____

_____

_____

_____

_____

_____

_____

_____

Let's Discuss

6. Do you feel support in the workplace from anyone?

_____

_____

_____

_____

_____

_____

_____

_____

_____

_____

_____

_____

Let's Discuss

7. Do you know a friend who experienced sexism/racism?

_____

_____

_____

_____

_____

_____

_____

_____

_____

_____

_____

_____

_____

Let's Discuss

8. When is it time to speak up?

_____

_____

_____

_____

_____

_____

_____

_____

_____

_____

_____

_____

Let's Discuss

9. Has your upbringing influenced how you believe you are to act in the workplace?

_____

_____

_____

_____

_____

_____

_____

_____

_____

_____

_____

_____

Let's Discuss

10. Do your friends and family believe your hostile work experiences?

_____

_____

_____

_____

_____

_____

_____

_____

_____

_____

_____

_____

Let's Discuss

11. Has discrimination in the workplace affected your mental health?

_____

_____

_____

_____

_____

_____

_____

_____

_____

_____

_____

_____

_____

Let's Discuss

12. Have you sought counseling over your workplace experience?

_____

_____

_____

_____

_____

_____

_____

_____

_____

_____

_____

_____

Let's Discuss

13. Have you experienced sexual harassment in the workplace?

_____

_____

_____

_____

_____

_____

_____

_____

_____

_____

_____

_____

Prompts with Purpose

1. Do you feel that you are valued at your current job? Remember, you are valuable regardless of this answer.

_____

_____

_____

_____

_____

_____

_____

_____

_____

_____

_____

_____

_____

_____

Prompts with Purpose

2. How have your work experiences impacted your mental health long term ?

_____

_____

_____

_____

_____

_____

_____

_____

_____

_____

_____

_____

_____

Prompts with Purpose

3. What are some actions that you can take to protect your mental health in the workplace? This could be anything from setting boundaries to moving positions.

_____

_____

_____

_____

_____

_____

_____

_____

_____

_____

_____

_____

THE INVISIBLE WOMAN'S
AFFIRMATION

I AM VALUABLE IN MY
PROFESSIONAL AND PERSONAL LIFE.

I AM DESERVING OF
PEACE AND RESPECT.

II:
TIME'S UP

Our Story

"YOU HAVE TO BE WILLING TO
CHOOSE YOURSELF OVER ANY
COMPANY, CAREER, OR MANAGER."

Monica

It can feel like you are against the world when you are at work, facing the dilemma of speaking up and rocking the boat. Thoughts of *"I'm the only one here and the only one who looks like me"* are common. If you start talking and shaking the ground, you're putting yourself at risk for them to bring someone in who looks just like them. A chance for them to prove that you don't belong. A chance for them to bring in someone they genuinely respect because, in all honesty, it isn't as if they really want you there in the first place. The only purpose for a person like you in a business like theirs is so they can check off their "diversity" box.

For months, I worked in a management-level position facing racial and gender discrimination. It was my peers, who were other managers for different cross-functional teams, who started to recognize that a particular executive always singled me out. He not only made me uncomfortable but them as well with the way he treated me. All of this lingered in the back of my mind, pushing me to contemplate leaving the job. I knew that once I voiced my concerns, I would have to move on. This is the caveat to speaking up. When you do, you must get ready to either leave the company or get pushed out. That is the consequence of being your own advocate. As Black women, we have it in us to advocate for ourselves and stick up for what we know to be right. However, there is always the consequence of getting pushed out and making the situation worse because of the intimidation factor. I did not speak up until my peer, who was a manager of another group, went and told HR that she felt uncomfortable because the executive made me uncomfortable. It was as if a lifeboat was sent my way. At that moment, I knew someone had my back in the company. Though I was already aware months prior that it would not work in my favor, at least I could finally set my mind free and say something.

Shortly after speaking up, I contacted my attorney, and I prepared for war. It was stressful, to say the least, but also heartbreaking. There is nothing worse than experiencing this and driving yourself crazy because you want to know why this is happening everywhere. *What am I doing?* You start to internalize. *Should I be doing something different?* You try various strategies and get the same results. You have no choice but to contact attorneys. One conversation with them confirms what you knew. You were exposed to a hostile racist, sexist environment. Melody and I both have an attorney on speed dial because of our separate yet similar experiences. You need a legal team to pinpoint specific implications and build your case. In this book, we are explaining it in layman's terms. They can get to the bottom of everything.

Melody

My first experience let me know I needed to do more than show documentation. I had to start conversations around these experiences. The patterns of behavior were becoming too noticeable. When it initially happened to me, my first thought was not to complain. As people say, you have to stay in your place. Follow the *"Don't ask, don't tell"* policy, but that didn't work for me. I knew the conversation needed to take place. I had to let someone know what I was seeing and how I was perceiving what was happening. The first conversation was with my boss. A conversation of this type is not always taken well because no one wants to be called out. Not that I used the word "racist," but even challenging their management of me in my career was too much. It immediately opened the floodgates for a hostile environment or some type of retaliation.

This is when I knew documentation was important because when it was time to go a step further with HR or to the next level of the management leadership team, I learned if it was not documented then it did not exist. Simply telling a story will present as just your feelings and emotions. Maybe you are looking at it wrong. You must have a track record and be ready to stack the deck and make people accountable. As I continued to go to the next jobs, I knew to start the documentation process as I saw the subtle situations that led to similar circumstances. I would advise that when you are on the job, keep a notebook on the side in case you have to document unfortunate events in the workplace. Write everything down. Nothing is too subtle to put on paper.

Our Truths

Monica

You have to be willing to choose yourself over any company, career, or manager. That is the truth you have to prepare in your head. You must be okay with the understanding that voicing your concerns will not end well. No matter how many seem to be on your side, no matter if you receive a promotion, the odds of you staying in the company are slim to none. I received a promotion and one of my bosses, who was supportive when my father passed away, was still not enough of a shield when his supervisor set out for blood. He worked to send me out of the company and when he accomplished his goal, everyone knew.

Before leaving, my boss told me in a private conversation: *"I really like you, but I'm very glad you are leaving because it is just too much."*

That hurt me to the core because this was another place where I became a manager and had high hopes that I would thrive and go on to the director level and excel.

"I'm going to have to leave this company" is a conversation that you *must* have with yourself in preparation for what is to come.

Tell yourself: *"I am going to stand for what is right because I am almost going insane coming to work each day experiencing this and no one knows it."*

It is an abuse suffered in silence. It leaves you feeling alone and helpless. Your peers do not know what you are experiencing. They cannot relate because they are white, Asian, and every other race. They're not walking around with a bull's eye on their back. You are. When it is time to fight back and experience the retaliation, you must prepare yourself. Tell yourself you are enough and you can do this. You have more support than you know. Other women out there have experienced this. You have a sister squad.

Melody

When I took the time to stop and observe the things I saw caucasian and Asian colleagues doing in my department that allowed them to excel, I noticed that the only difference was the color of my skin. I have the education and that is great. However, depending on who my manager was, having an education was null and void. For Black women, you have to work quicker, harder and have every skillset from A-Z. Depending on who your manager is, they may feel it is nice that you have all of those bells and whistles but they don't need that.

So you think, *"Let me start inserting myself on projects to become more visible."*

Black women in many cases feel invisible in the workplace. So what are we to do? I showed more and kept my head down but still was observant enough to notice what I needed to do. When I did I got great results on my performance review all across the board with no issues. But I was still not seeing the acceleration of my career that I saw with my racial counterparts. I knew I needed to take a step toward having a discussion with the boss.

One day I spoke to the project manager: *"Hey there was a project you told me I would be put on because it would be high visibility to the CEO and the leadership team that could definitely lead to promotion."*

He said, *"Yes I heard and thought you were going to get on the project. When I went directly to your boss* (who was a white woman), *she told me she had changed her mind. She felt like she did not want you to be on that project because you were handling too many other things, and she wanted you to just focus on one."*

I was shocked and taken aback because I think being able to multitask, be diverse, show all of my expertise, and be successful is a one-up for me. Other women do that and move up. Why did she not tell me this? Why was I not given the same opportunity? That was an issue for me, and I saw she truly did not want me to excel.

Her roadblocks did not stop there. My efforts to be visible were also sabotaged. After many restless nights, I finally decided that I would take matters into my own hands and not allow my manager to stifle my career growth. I reached out to a Black woman who held a leadership role in a cross-functional team I worked with closely. I had crossed paths with this sister and seen her lead presentations in our company-wide meetings. This Black woman displayed humble yet boss-lady vibes, and she was someone I wanted to get career advice from. I wanted to know what the "secret sauce" was to navigating this organization that didn't have many executives who looked like us. In my next meeting with my manager, I mentioned to her that I had a meet-and-greet with her counterpart.

She gave me a side eye and said, *"That's nice."*

At that moment, I knew she didn't approve of the fact I was trying to be seen and heard to move on and up from her leadership.

I started looking for opportunities to move into another department in the organization's finance area. I figured I needed to get from under her leadership because clearly there was an issue. I decided to go back to school to obtain my MBA, and that did not sit right with her. All she did was question my decision.

"Are you sure this is what you want to do? Do you think your husband is going to be supportive?" She asked very personal questions with very negative undertones. It was discouraging and distracted me from even wanting to pursue it.

I thought, *"Would she have asked a white woman all of these questions? Would she have asked a male that?"*

Her nerve to ask me those inappropriate questions blew my mind. Did she really see me furthering my career as an issue? The more I saw myself trying to excel the way I saw other women excelling, the results of success and greatness were not happening for me. I could not help but acknowledge there was a problem. It was not about gender because the department was full of females, but I was the only Black female. It all trickled down to race. I went to HR and from there I reached out to legal counsel because I refused to allow one bad apple to determine my succession and career in the company.

Common Myths

COMMON MYTH:

Black women don't have the skills to lead. Therefore, they deserve lesser pay than their counterparts.

TRUTH:

When you think of equitable pay, the idea is that you pay someone where they are. When talking in terms of Black women in equal pay, equity is paying me what you pay a man. Equitability is meeting the Black woman where she is but not underpaying her and making sure she is getting paid the same fair amount for the same work that her white male colleagues are doing.

The Real Truth

Monica

Research shows that when we go into professional spaces, we have to work twice as hard as a white or Asian person to get and maintain the same job role. So, for example, you want to go into management? You must be seven years-plus into your career to even be considered for a managerial position versus a white or Asian person who is young and right out of college or may have worked only one or two years in their career. With that research alone, it already tells us that Black women must work harder and faster to simply get a position.

Feeling as if you are not good enough for a position is one thing, but knowing you are not good enough simply because of the color of your skin is crushing to the core. You get questioned on whether you are qualified for a job or not despite your experience showing that you are. You line yourself up against white or Asian counterparts and you start at the same level with the same accolades, but they do not get asked those same questions. For one of my podcasts, I mentioned a boss saying to me that I knew the dictionary and the English language very well and I was very articulate. I was taken aback. How insulting. Just because I am Black, you are impressed by how well I know the English language? This is the only language I am supposed to know.

Melody

Know your worth and be secure in yourself that all bets are on you. You are putting all your cards on the table. This is a conversation you must have with yourself, no matter what comes with it. The feeling of triumph and excitement that you are going to stand up for yourself and call this situation out overwhelms you when you make this affirmation. You believe everything will be taken care of and all will be well. Know that 99% of the time, the situation does not go that way. What I have seen for myself and in many others' stories is that most of the time your colleagues are possibly going to turn their backs on you because they do not want to be involved or risk their jobs. Even with HR, though they send you nice and sweet emails like they are standing up for you, they are more for the leadership team and the company.

Acknowledging there is racism in a situation does not automatically mean sexism will also be acknowledged. You have to fight that to the last straw to prove it. At that point, you are a liability. For myself, the heaviness of it all led to depression and issues in my personal relationships. You go home and it is still on your mind. You don't just drop it off when you leave the workplace. You either talk about it too much or you do not talk about it enough. You repress it and you feel it. It shows and is written all over your face. Knowing your world can possibly be turned upside down almost breaks you. On the flip side, you are getting ready to leave a toxic work environment, which is similar to when you leave an unhealthy relationship. It may not go well and not everybody will like it because no one wants to be called the bad apple. You have to know your worth and what will be the best decision for you. It may mean changing jobs, but you have to be ready for whatever change will come. It could mean leaving the field and similar environments altogether because not everyone will acknowledge there is a problem or be willing to change their behavior. You have to choose yourself.

LET'S EXAMINE

ANALYZING GENDER AND RACE IN THE WORKPLACE

1. No Girls Allowed: Exposing Male-Dominated Positions and Pay

35% of women make up senior leadership positions despite making up 54.3% of the workforce.

Ariella, Sky. "25 Women in Leadership Statistics [2022]: Facts on the Gender Gap in Corporate and Political Leadership." *Zippia 25 Women In Leadership Statistics 2022 Facts On The Gender Gap In Corporate And Political Leadership Comments*, Zippia, 19 Apr. 2022, www.zippia.com.

Despite the fact that women constitute a large part of the workforce, there are still a number of careers and industries dominated by men. Although these numbers are changing, the results are still slow. Among women born between 1980 and 1984, the U.S. Bureau of Labor Statistics (BLS) found they were more likely than their male peers to have completed a bachelor's degree by the age of 31 ("Women More Likely"). Opportunities for traditionally male jobs increase as women become more educated. Fields such as construction, farmers, engineers, pastors, architects, and firefighters remain male-dominated ("Women in Male-Dominated"). There was a lawsuit filed against Google for gender bias in 2017 that was settled in 2022 (Thomas). Three former female Google employees found out that male colleagues were being placed in higher positions than them despite similar qualifications. This led to them being paid less. An attorney from San Francisco filed a lawsuit alleging Google pays women less than men systemically. The company highlighted a move it took to eliminate the gender pay gap. When discussing wages with their employers, California workers are protected from retaliation.

In addition to implicit and explicit bias in the workplace, gender differences in the way credit is given and differences in the way men and women negotiate are factors that explain the gender earnings gap. Gender diversity in the workplace is important for many reasons. In most industries, however, there is a limited amount of information available on the possibility that increasing the number of women in the workplace would help reduce the gender wage gap. It is possible that women may never be exposed to traditionally masculine careers due to socialized ideas about what is considered men's work and what is considered women's work. By organizing unions and gaining a voice on behalf of their fellow employees, women can help settle the unfair advantage men have in many different industries. In spite of companies' investment in mentoring and developing their female talent pool, promotions are not always a result. The 2008 Catalyst survey found that more women than men had mentors, but those mentors had less access to organizational decision-making ("Women in Male-Dominated"). Since 2008, the promotion rate for men has increased by 15% despite all the efforts to develop women. In the men's case, lateral moves resulted in promotions. In the women's case, lateral moves were available in lieu of promotions. The mentoring relationships women have aren't resulting in nearly as many promotions as they would have if they were men. There is still a perception within society that women are less likely to get jobs in male-dominated positions. It is particularly hard for women to excel in industries or occupations that are dominated by men because of harmful stereotypes and unfavorable work environments. In 2020, there were only 6.5% of full-time women in male-dominated jobs in the United States ("Women in Male-Dominated). Women working in male-dominated industries face a variety of challenges, including limitations set by societal expectations and beliefs about women in leadership positions, higher stress and anxiety levels, lack of mentoring and career promotions, and sexual harassment.

2. International Affairs: Exploring Pay Equity Abroad

On average, women only earn 68% of what men are paid in the same work field globally.

McCarthy, Joe. "What Is the Gender Pay Gap and How Do We Close It?" *Global Citizen*, Global Poverty Project, Inc., 11 Mar. 2021, www.globalcitizen.org.

The theme of 2022's International Women's Day is #BreakTheBias, which invites us to envision a world free of prejudice, stereotypes, and discrimination. A number of legislative initiatives and workplace movements have been implemented around the world to eliminate workplace bias at various points throughout a woman's career. We will review some of the disparities that women face throughout their careers utilizing Payscale's *Gender Pay Gap Report* released for Equal Pay Day on March 15, 2022, and legislation aimed at reducing pay gaps.

Women who have achieved the same career status as men earn $0.99 for every dollar earned by men (McCarthy). This is known as the controlled gender pay gap, which can be even worse for different groups based on racial or ethnic background. For every dollar a man makes, women in their 30s earn $0.98 (McCarthy). Black women's income gaps are even wider. Despite equal pay laws existing for more than 50 years, worldwide reporting requirements are being introduced now to help close the pay gap. Organizations are voluntarily reporting pay equity as part of transparency programs for Environmental, Social, and Governance (ESG) or because there is an expectation from employees. In 90 countries around the world, there is Equal Pay for Equal Value legislation that ensures that no matter the number of women in a role, if the role is of equal value, they must be paid equally. In Canada, legislation requires employers to report pay data for gendered roles.

There is often secrecy surrounding the recruitment process and payment information is rarely disclosed. There are a number of pay transparency laws in New York City and Colorado, as well as proposed legislation in the EU designed to remove trying to figure this information out without any data. By requiring pay ranges with job postings, these new laws ensure that all potential employees will start on the same footing. Promotions and/or advancements are also subject to this requirement under the proposed legislation, such as California's new pay transparency law, Senate Bill 1162. It may not be as simple as it seems to pass pay transparency laws in some states, given that prospective and current employees will see the posted pay ranges. There will be a lot of disgruntled employees if organizations do not create pay structures they are confident of and can easily explain. Under proposed EU legislation and in some countries like Iceland, France, and Germany, current reporting requirements require companies to establish pay structures that enable employees of equal value to be compared with each other. Developing formal pay structures and analyzing them for equity ensures that any bias that currently exists is reduced. As employees change jobs within and between organizations, this legislation is intended to reduce bias.

Research shows that women are more likely than men to take career breaks. Pay structures will ensure that women re-entering the workforce will be less likely to be penalized for taking time off. It is possible for employees to fall behind in their pay during maternity leave, even if they remain with the organization. In order to rectify this, France is requiring transparency on whether female employees returning from maternity or adoption leave benefited from a pay increase similar to their male colleagues who were not on leave. Legislation and reporting requirements from around the world may eventually persuade organizations to investigate their own data for improvement, even if laws don't demand such introspection. Employee expectations of pay equity are on the rise, and proactive stances like these are increasingly viewed as key talent strategies. A company's ability to break biases will distinguish it as an honest, equal employer in today's labor market.

3. Babies, Business, and Bouncing Back

As of 2021, 81.2% of employed mothers with children 6 to 17 work full time, compared to 77.2% of mothers with children less than 6.

"Employment Characteristics of Families - 2021." *U.S. Bureau of Labor Statistics*, 20 Apr. 2022, www.bls.gov.

Women's pay gaps begin small but can grow significantly due to prior salary disclosure, leave requirements, and lack of promotions throughout their careers. One final element is the woman's choice of work when she also has caregiving responsibilities or her decision to not join the workforce altogether. The pandemic has brought this issue to light. A study by McKinsey & Company found that about two million women, primarily mothers with young children, have been forced to consider leaving the workforce or taking a step back from their careers due to the COVID-19 crisis (Ellingrud). In the UK, a study by the Institute for Fiscal Studies found that women took care of their families more during the pandemic, regardless of whether they earned a higher wage ("Women Much More"). Women are either out of the labor force or in the labor force but in a lower-paying role that they are over-qualified for, thus further increasing the earnings gap over their lifetime. It's possible there are some brilliant primary caregiver fathers as well, but it is likely that women will continue to bear the brunt of childcare without adequate legislation and employer policies. The researchers found the provision of equal paternity leave and more equal access to quality affordable childcare were two of the most important measures for increasing female participation in the workforce. As part of the proposed California pay transparency law, Senate Bill 1162, employers are asked to report their leave policies and ensure consideration of how the policies impact those with caring responsibilities ("California SB 1162").

In addition to raising their family, starting and running businesses, maintaining part-time or full-time employment, taking care of elderly loved ones, battling infertility, nurturing pregnancies, losing their job and so much more, many mothers have also had to roll up their sleeves. According to 2021 Census Bureau and Bureau of Labor Statistics data, about 3.5 million mothers living with school-aged children left active work between March and April 2020, either shifting into paid or unpaid leave, losing their jobs, or quitting the workforce altogether (Heggeness). Mothers were shifted to unpaid work for two main reasons: They were more likely to work in service-oriented jobs that were impacted heavily by the pandemic, and they bore the heavier burden of caregiving duties such as housework and childcare (Heggeness). Due to gender inequality at home and at work, mothers have always worked in a V-shaped pattern, with a downward and upward cycle that affects their promotion, advancement, and income (Heggeness). Throughout the world, women of all ages and from all walks of life are making the decision to leave their jobs to care for their children. We will never reach gender parity until women stop doing housework on a daily basis and men start helping around the house. Taking care of the children, cooking, and handling household chores affects a mother's productivity at work, making it more difficult to perform the job with the same focus and intensity as men. Families in the United States continue to suffer the impact of a fractured society that has placed capitalism above the well-being of working families.

4. Say It Loud: I'm Black, and I'm Proud

In the U.S., 65% of employees are satisfied with their jobs, with 20% being passionate about their jobs.

"11 Surprising Job Satisfaction Statistics (2022)." Apollo Technical LLC, 14 Feb. 2022, www.apollotechnical.com.

If you want to be happy in your job, you have to feel a sense of belonging. This is also crucial for your employer as well, because when employees feel a part of something, they are more likely to stay, succeed, and be brand ambassadors. To foster a greater sense of belonging for employees of color, corporate America will need to examine how racism has played a role in hiring, work assignments, promotions, and pay. A study from 2020 by the Coqual–formerly known as the Center for Talent Innovation, which advises mainly Fortune 500 companies on diversity and inclusion–found white employees report a greater sense of belonging than their Black, Hispanic, or Asian counterparts (Kennedy). Feeling seen, feeling connected, feeling supported, and feeling proud are the four broad categories measured in the study. Upper-management has an important role in making sure everyone has a sense of belonging. Barack Obama's election as president in 2008 was viewed as proof that the color of one's skin would no longer limit people from attaining important leadership roles in the United States. However, Black executives did not feel this way and faced racial and pay issues in the workplace as they moved up in the company. Despite the rising number of African Americans earning bachelor's and graduate degrees, Black people are still scarce and stagnant in management and senior executive positions. In many companies, discussing race and equal pay is taboo, and business leaders often stay quiet about it. It is a cloak of silence that enfolds the whole organization.

The strategy adopted by many young Black professionals seeking to advance to senior leadership positions is to remain silent about race and inequality to avoid being branded troublemakers and being overlooked for advancement opportunities. Study results by Sylvia Ann Hewlett and colleagues in 2017 found that 78% of Black professionals had experienced discrimination or were afraid that they or their loved ones would, yet 38% felt it was unacceptable to speak about bias at their workplaces ("Diversity Joint" 8-10). By diffusing the topic, African American workers may feel companies are unwilling to address their concerns and their talent is being undervalued or squandered. This can lead to a reduction in their engagement with colleagues, satisfaction with their work, and loyalty to their companies. In an attempt to recruit and retain more minorities, many organizations have created diversity and inclusion programs. Companies can start using data analytics to report whether their employees feel included on their teams and are treated fairly. Furthermore, companies should make an effort to train managers on how to dispose of racial bias in their hiring and recruitment processes. Additionally, they should invest in hiring more Black professionals, in part by reinforcing the message that race will not be a barrier to advancement. This is greatly important today at a time when inclusion programs have shifted toward recognizing more forms of diversity that are based on gender and sexual orientation. Employers need to make sure discussions about race are not getting lost as they work to make a better workplace where everyone feels like they belong.

5. To Work or Not To Work, That Is The Question

In 2020, 2.3 million people left the American workforce.

Ellingrud, Kweilin. "What We Lose When We Lose Women in the Workforce." *McKinsey & Company*, 3 June 2021, www.mckinsey.com.

A new study from Lean In and McKinsey & Company shows that women are more likely than men to feel burned out ("Women in the Workplace"). This disparity may cause more women to consider downshifting their careers or leaving them altogether. The study finds that 1 in 3 women have considered changing or leaving their jobs in the past year, compared with 1 in 4 women in 2020 ("Women in the Workplace"). Men and women both say they feel burned out compared with 2020, and there is nearly a doubled difference between the percentage of women who are burned out compared to men. Although there has been increased attention to diversity and inclusion issues, the *Women in the Workplace* report found that women of color are still experiencing microaggressions about the same as they did before the pandemic. Mothers working outside the home are juggling work responsibilities with family obligations to make it all look easy. Before the COVID-19 crisis, it appeared some progress was being made in the workplace. However, many mothers are still wrestling with the question of whether to work or not. Single mothers fight with a "double shift" of working a job along with household responsibilities, mental health challenges, a more difficult remote-work experience, and concerns about higher rates of unemployment. This is compounded in the African American and minority communities.

Employers can retain employees most affected by the pandemic if they adapt to becoming more flexible and empathetic in the workplace. Moreover, they can cultivate a culture that encourages all working mothers to maximize their potential. Many companies have adopted a flexible work schedule with the option to work remotely to make returning to the office seamless.

According to McKinsey & Company, 2.3 million women dropped out of the workforce in 2020 (Ellingrud). Women with children do want to return to the workplace but are challenged with virtual school, daycare closures, lack of childcare, and increased childcare needs. The number of Americans quitting their jobs is on the rise (Parker). We are now in the Great Resignation era, which illustrates a long-simmering issue that has boiled over the last two years: Workers are looking for more from their careers, especially Black workers. There has been a spotlight on why Black professionals are leaving the corporate workforce to become entrepreneurs. According to an article by Jasmine Browley, a 2022 LinkedIn survey of 1,001 Black entrepreneurs showed that 48% of people shared the motivating factor was financial, 46% included the need for flexibility and more remote work options, 34% said more free time, and lack of fulfillment at a previous job was at 30% (Browley). In addition, 37% of Black entrepreneurs with full-time jobs feel they have been overlooked for career advancement opportunities because they have their own business, while 55% of Black entrepreneurs left the workforce to have more control over their lives (Browley). According to an article by Patricia Worthy for the *Guardian*, a study by Working Mother Research Institute showed that 52% of Black women were actively considering leaving their workplaces within two years (Worthy). Finances were severely impacted by the pandemic for women of color. The number of Black women who have been laid off, furloughed, or whose hours or pay have been reduced is almost double that of white men (Worthy). The financial hurdles combined with hostile racial work environments are among the reasons Black women leave corporate America and start their own company.

6. Legal Privilege

Only 30% of employees who face harassment based on gender, age, race, and sexuality, national origin, or disability file internal complaints, with less than 15% filing formal legal charges.

Zheng, Lily. "Do Your Employees Feel Safe Reporting Abuse and Discrimination?" *Harvard Business Review*, Harvard Business School Publishing, 8 Oct. 2020, hbr.org.

In no way does a gender pay gap mean that an employer has failed to adhere to the Equality Act 2010's equal pay obligations. Nevertheless, this new obligation to publish pay information will most likely draw attention to the issue of equal pay. Some trade unions may start examining companies' pay policies to determine if there are any potential equal pay issues. If an employee decides to bring a legal claim against the company, they may attempt to obtain documentation created by the business of its complying with gender pay gap reporting obligations. This could be in the hope of supporting a legal argument that the company has breached its equal pay obligations. Unless the documents are protected by legal professional privilege, they can be disclosed. An employer's denial to provide copies of this information without good reason may lead to adverse consequences. Legal privilege is good for these purposes. Legal privilege protects from leaking confidential communications between clients and their legal team. It ensures the clients will be able to obtain legal advice in confidence without fear of retaliation. There are two types of legal privilege: Legal advice privilege that protects confidentiality and litigation privilege that applies when litigation has started or is contemplated. A document is not privileged simply because it is stated as such, and not all communications are protected. If you need legal privilege, please talk in detail with your legal team.

All employees are affected by pay equity, from new hires who seek a fair employer to seasoned executives who want to attract and keep talent that stimulates innovation. If some groups are excluded from higher-paying leadership roles, any imbalance in workforce representation needs to be addressed. The level of education, experience, and responsibilities of individuals must also be accounted for when designing an equitable pay structure. The Federal Pay Act law has many loopholes, and the definition has since evolved, with many states writing their own independent pay equity laws. In the context of workplace investigations, particularly before any lawsuit is filed, the applicability of certain privileges is a complex issue. Whenever an attorney conducts an investigation or provides direction to a non-attorney, there are usually questions regarding whether the investigation is discoverable or protected by a particular law. When these privileges do apply and employers raise the adequacy of their investigation and/or corrective action, they may lose these legal privilege protections. Once they are lost, investigative materials may become subject to disclosure during the discovery process. The attorney-client privilege, the oldest privilege known under common law, protects the communications between an attorney and client regarding information related to legal representation. Attorneys are called upon by employers and employees to facilitate investigations of workplace misconduct. Employers can commit a large variety of illegal actions that can place employees at a disadvantage and/or violate their rights. You should contact an employment attorney in any of the following situations:

- You have been or are being harassed at work.
- You have been discriminated against because of race, gender, pregnancy, etc.
- You are facing retaliation for exercising a right you are entitled to by law.
- Your employment has been terminated and that act is in violation of your rights.
- You have been denied certain benefits that you are entitled to.

1. Equal Pay Deficits Across Industries

Men earn $10,381 more than women in 2022.

Wheelwright, Trevor. "The Gender Pay Gap across the US in 2022." *Business.org*, 1 Mar. 2022.

The gender pay deficit has been expressed as cents to the dollar according to what women make versus men. A persistent pay gap between men and women continues to hurt our nation's workers and our economy over half a century after pay discrimination was banned. The equal pay deficit even follows women into retirement. As a result of lower lifetime earnings, women receive less in Social Security and pensions than their male counterparts (Wheelwright). Women have only 70% of what men do in overall retirement income ("The Simple Truth"). Experts expect the gender pay gap to widen because of the economic downside of Covid-19. Women face a persistent pay gap deficit in nearly every industry, with a greater discrepancy in some fields.

According to a CNBC article by Morgan Smith, there are a few industries that stand out as having the largest gender pay gaps, most of which have a higher percentage of working women than men:

1. Finance and insurance
2. Agencies and consultancies
3. Health care
4. Transportation and warehousing
5. Nonprofits

Industries with the smallest gender pay gaps:

1. Arts, entertainment, and recreation

2. Real estate and rental/leasing

3. Construction

4. Technology

5. Education

Industries with equal pay or more than men:

1. Sewing machine operators

2. Food prep and service workers

3. Teacher assistants

4. Counselors

5. Transportation and distribution

6. Stock clerks and order fillers

7. Physical therapists

8. Receptionists

9. Sales

In all industries combined, women make 83% of what men do, according to the Bureau of Labor Statistics (Iacurci). Despite differences in job types, job levels, training, education, work hours, and location, women still earn less than men. This is due to bias in the workplace. The equal pay deficit cannot be blamed on any singular factor. There are a host of obstacles women face that add to this pay shortfall, such as caregiving expectations that limit women's hours at work and the amount of time men spend at home. There are also pay gains that disappear as women age, wage differences between male and female jobs, and wage discrimination against women and minorities. Over the decades, women have entered the workforce in record-breaking numbers and have made great strides in educational attainment. However, when compared to men, women are still paid less, are likely to have low-wage jobs, and are more likely to live in poverty. Gender wage discrimination is present at nearly all wage levels, occupations, and industries ("The Simple Truth"). Closing the gender wage gap across all industries is necessary for helping women achieve financial and economic security. To bring true financial security to American women, more must be done. Additionally, the gender wage gap has continued and hourly wage growth has stalled. This is the result of intentional policy decisions that have stopped the vast majority of workers from securing higher wages. Women of color are continuously disproportionately affected by wage inequalities. Wages for the vast majority of labor workers have been stagnant since the 1970s, increasing drastically slower than the rate of productivity increased (Lee). Maximizing women's economic security will require closing the gender wage gap and enacting policies to raise wages and reverse racial and gender inequality.

Caveat: Ring The Alarm

Monica

We want to share with Black women that you should never marry a job you date. Even though we deal with discrimination and unfair treatment on a day-to-day job, there may be a boss out there who treats you the way you need to be treated. A boss who pays you what you are worth and gives you what you are asking for. Don't get stuck on one particular company. You might find yourself moving around quite a bit, but sometimes you have to do that for your sanity. Know that it's ok to do so.

Companies will now be forced to try to retain Black women. To those companies, know that it is good to hire Black women, but don't hire Black women for diversity clout. If you are going to hire a Black woman, especially a woman with many years of experience or who has been in management or higher roles, you need to make sure you include her in everything that comes along with that. This includes, but is not limited to, meetings, introducing her to cross-functional teams and training. Though jobs may not officially train, we have learned that other nationalities, especially white males going into jobs, do receive a sort of unofficial training through mentorship or outside sources. Black women should also receive similar training when they come on board. Again, it's not just enough to hire a Black woman for diversity clout. You have to make sure you are being inclusive in the environment. Trust that a woman knows how to do her job and give her the support she needs to really fit the role.

Melody

As Black women, we are speaking up and showing up for ourselves more than ever. We understand our value and we are no longer afraid to leave. Even during the pandemic, many Black workers, specifically women, left their corporate workplaces to become entrepreneurs or moved on to other roles where they would be valued (Worthy). No longer are we afraid to leave organizations where we feel we are not treated fairly, respected, or valued. More companies are scrambling to figure out strategies to retain Black women employees. Black women in those environments are good workers and contributors but are not acknowledged or rewarded. We predict that more companies will see drastic changes in their workforce regarding Black women. No longer are we sitting around for 20 to 30 years, regardless of the circumstances. We are leaving and doing so at drastic rates. Companies will have to put their money where their mouth is. They will have to take action and live up to what they said they would do during the times of George Floyd and Brianna Taylor. They must invest in their Black talent.

Companies must also give Black women power. In some cases, Black women may get the VP role or the head of some diversity role, but if you do not give them the power and allow them the room to make decisions, then it is null. There is no reason to put them in the role if you're not going to let them do what you hired them to do.

Final Commentary

Monica

We are speaking up for ourselves. No longer are we tolerating the days of our parents who worked in corporations and just showed up and smiled while dealing with harassment to protect their job and family. Now Black women are being much more creative than ever. We are skyrocketing in the rate of becoming entrepreneurs because we are getting tired of being mistreated (Worthy). We have a voice and we are using it.

Melody

Black women now demand to be seen, heard, and valued, and we are not taking "No" for an answer. We are not waiting for someone to come and save us or advocate for our behalf. We are doing it for ourselves and we are doing it in record numbers. We are coming together in large groups to advocate, sponsor, and support one another, and that's what this book is about.

CASE STUDY

SHANNON POWER, VP OF FINANCE

1. HAVE YOU EVER FELT LIKE YOU HAD TO BE QUIET ABOUT DISCRIMINATION YOU FACED IN THE WORKPLACE IN ORDER TO ADVANCE?

Yes, especially where I am at now. It is a small world and there aren't many women, which is why I am extremely passionate about gender equality in corporate leadership. Every important decision about your career is made in rooms you are not in. Having women in those spaces is critical. When faced recently with pay discrimination in the workplace, I had the choice of keeping quiet and being promoted–which puts more women into those leadership positions–or speaking up. The choice becomes a question of if I can live without speaking up and will that choice be better for women in the workplace in the long run?

2. IN THE LAST TWO YEARS, DID YOU PARTICIPATE IN THE GREAT RESIGNATION ERA AND IF SO, WHY?

I personally was not part of the great resignation, although I did switch jobs about a year- and-a-half ago. However, I do know several people who have participated in the great resignation. Many of those folks tell me that it is really about moving from a toxic work culture into one that is less toxic. The pressure of the pandemic pushed people into action. Something had to give. There ended up being a lot of opportunities to move to cultures that were not so toxic and many people took the opportunity.

3. DO YOU FEEL THAT THE CORPORATE WORLD PREVENTS WOMEN FROM GETTING PREGNANT OR MAKES IT DIFFICULT FOR THEM TO BALANCE FAMILY AND WORK LIFE?

Yes. The corporate world is not built for women and definitely not built for women who would like to have children. It's for career-focused men who have someone at home to take care of the children. That is why it is so important for us to come together with our allies and re-engineer the system. It's not broken. It is working exactly as it was intended to. We instead need to re-engineer it. This includes learning to advocate for ourselves and our needs in the workplace, which tends to be reactive rather than proactive.

4. DO YOU FEEL THAT THE LAW DOES ENOUGH TO PROTECT WOMEN FROM WORKPLACE DISCRIMINATION?

No, and one key piece of the law that I would like to see removed are non-disclosure agreements. The Me Too movement really highlighted many of the issues with NDAs in the workplace. As long as companies are allowed to use the NDA to silence women and people of color for discrimination and harassment that goes on, then we'll never know truly how widespread, rampant, and bad discrimination in the workplace really is. It's challenging for victims because they can't tell their story without legal repercussions. How are we supposed to be our full authentic selves if we can't tell our stories? Many people who sign NDAs do it early on in their careers. They are young, naive, preyed upon, and the company they work for ends up having power over them. If we were to eliminate NDAs, I think it would be eye-opening for a lot of people. If NDAs went away, companies would be held more accountable for their actions and the cultures that they either participate in or turn a blind eye to.

CASE STUDY

DR. KHALID WHITE

It is my core belief that sharing our history and culture will change the world. I have dedicated my professional career to the field of African American studies. My passion for teaching, learning and telling our stories drives me.

I completed my undergrad studies in Sociology at Morehouse College. During my time there, I realized how crucial education is to changing lives, changing narratives and to uplifting communities.

While continuing my education journey at Harvard Univ. & UC Davis, I took pride in studying Education and African American studies.

Being an educator continues to be a privilege and I love it. BLKMPWR builds on that love and is dedicated to changing the narrative about the Black community.

With BLKMPWR, I'm educating outside of the traditional classroom space. Using books, film, fashion, music and technology to educate, inspire and empower.

WHAT ARE YOUR THOUGHTS ON THE HISTORICAL CONTEXT OF EQUITY IN PAY FOR BLACK PEOPLE?

Black families had been torn and ripped apart from 1619 on, culminating in generational trauma that continues to be passed on. That includes sexual violence and physical abuse. To be quite honest, the Equity Pay Gap is part of that generational trauma as well. If your grandmother or great-grandmother scrubbed floors or were out in the field for no pay, that impacts us today. Now, when you're in your cubicle in the air conditioning, you're at a job that you're supposed to want to be at, but you still feel like you are being undervalued and underappreciated because of the color of your skin, how your hair looks, among other things.

A white man working in the next cubicle makes more money than you make even though you are smarter than him and work just as hard. That trauma is passed down to your kids, then their kids, and so forth. Black men and women have generational trauma that continues to this day. A Black woman may have seen what her grandmother and mother had to do to make ends meet and internalized that. Her parents and grandparents had to do things, like working another job on the side, to make ends meet. That generational trauma comes with the wage gap and opportunity gap.

Let's Discuss

1. Which industry is the hardest for women to break into?

_____

_____

_____

_____

_____

_____

_____

_____

_____

_____

_____

_____

Let's Discuss

2. Should you speak up for others?

_____

_____

_____

_____

_____

_____

_____

_____

_____

_____

_____

_____

Let's Discuss

3. Does the corporate world hold back women?

_____

_____

_____

_____

_____

_____

_____

_____

_____

_____

_____

_____

Let's Discuss

4. When was your first experience with sexism/racism?

Let's Discuss

5. Were you afraid to speak up?

_____

_____

_____

_____

_____

_____

_____

_____

_____

_____

_____

_____

_____

Let's Discuss

6. Is sexism/racism a part of the job?

_____

_____

_____

_____

_____

_____

_____

_____

_____

_____

_____

_____

_____

Let's Discuss

7. Is self-respect or your career more important?

_____

_____

_____

_____

_____

_____

_____

_____

_____

_____

_____

_____

_____

Let's Discuss

8. Is the corporate world culture toxic?

_____

_____

_____

_____

_____

_____

_____

_____

_____

_____

_____

_____

_____

Let's Discuss

9. Do women contribute to the toxic culture?

_____

_____

_____

_____

_____

_____

_____

_____

_____

_____

_____

_____

_____

Let's Discuss

10. Would you file a lawsuit against your employer ?

_____

_____

_____

_____

_____

_____

_____

_____

_____

_____

_____

_____

Let's Discuss

11. Is the corporate world male dominated?

_____

_____

_____

_____

_____

_____

_____

_____

_____

_____

_____

_____

_____

_____

Let's Discuss

12. Does the corporate world prevent women from starting families?

_____

_____

_____

_____

_____

_____

_____

_____

_____

_____

_____

_____

Let's Discuss

13. Do you know of your legal rights in the workplace?

_____

_____

_____

_____

_____

_____

_____

_____

_____

_____

_____

_____

Let's Discuss

14. Does the law go far enough to protect women in the workplace?

_____

_____

_____

_____

_____

_____

_____

_____

_____

_____

_____

_____

Prompts with Purpose

1. Do you feel supported at your workplace? How about in your personal life?

_____

_____

_____

_____

_____

_____

_____

_____

_____

_____

_____

_____

_____

_____

Prompts with Purpose

2. What improvements could your workplace make to better support you? When your workplace lacks these qualities, how does that impact you and your mental health?

_____

_____

_____

_____

_____

_____

_____

_____

_____

_____

_____

_____

Prompts with Purpose

3. How can you add self-care practices into your work day and afterward?

_____

_____

_____

_____

_____

_____

_____

_____

_____

_____

_____

_____

_____

THE INVISIBLE WOMAN'S
AFFIRMATION

I AM THE BEST FOR MY JOB.
I GO AFTER WHAT I WANT. I
HAVE THE POWER TO CREATE
MY OWN SUCCESS.

III:
THE
EQUAL PAY
MOVEMENT

Our Story

"YOU CAN PULL A SEAT UP TO THE TABLE BUT IF YOU DO NOT HAVE A VOICE WHEN YOU GET THERE, IT DOES NOT MAKE ANY DIFFERENCE."

Monica

It was in 2016, and I was a senior billing manager at a tech company. I had a new CFO who came on board and gave me hell right off the bat. He did not like me and made sure life was difficult for me. He didn't want me in the role because I was a woman and I was a woman of color. I remember going through the harassment and at some point, I went to human resources. I remember talking to Melody over the phone, and I was crying. She told me not to worry and assured me that we would get through this. I remember us saying we're not the only ones who experience torment at work. These experiences are not very encouraging because your career is your bread and butter.

I remember at that moment saying to Melody, *"You have experience in the film industry. Why not make this into a documentary?"*

I wanted to film the process and the struggle from start to finish so that we could share our experience with the world. So right at that moment, Melody shared my sentiment, and that is how our documentary was born.

When we started on this journey, we thought it would be easy. We had the money and believed we could find someone trustworthy to film. We began our search with people of diverse backgrounds who worked in HR and who could give statistics validating what we knew. Our intent was not to get on camera and bash companies. Our goal has always been to provide vital information to validate our story. We didn't realize it would be as difficult as it was. Melody and I cofounded The Equal Balance Movement after filiming our documentary and hearing the mentions of Black Women finding out how underpaid they were along with experism racism on the job. EBM is a resource and safe space for women of color to locate resources and find community to help them navigate the conversation of being underpaid on the job. Our documentary represents what I mentioned in my life as the starting over. When you look at the big picture, it seems easy to attain. There are moments when you have to start over. It doesn't mean you're not going to get there. We started over with filming and editing and tried to get more people on deck to help build out the film. We kept our faith in God because there were moments when we wanted to throw it all out. After all, we questioned whether or not the idea was too grand. However, we pushed through, and God made a way.

Our first premiere in Oakland, California, was received very well, and that was the beginning of feeling very confident. It was the start of knowing we have something based on the feedback of viewers.

Young Black men tell us, *"I've seen my mom go through that while I was growing up."*

People feel connected to our story, and that lets us know we have a message for women and girls who look like us to help them get through it and heal. We want to help the young girls behind us who want to be corporate executives succeed. Our message to them is that they can, even with the trials and tribulations.

We wanted our documentary to be about the lack of representation. The lack of diversity happens everywhere but specifically in Silicon Valley with tech companies and reputable Fortune 500 companies where Black people are consumers and contribute heavily to their bottom line but are not represented as leaders and decision-makers. There is a lack of Black women when it comes to corporate leadership roles. However, there isn't a shortage when it comes to human resources/customer service. In 2019, only 0.8% of Fortune 500 companies had Black CEOs and Black men and women only made up 3.2% of all large company leadership roles across the U.S (Brooks). When you start to dice it out, men are often in leadership roles because they're engineers. I think my experience with the lack of diversity didn't allow me to show up as my authentic self. With the social injustices we've seen, companies are now laying the foundation to enable us to show up in our truth. As Black people, we often assimilate into corporate America with code-switching. This becomes very taxing. We are trying to teach women how to be individual contributors and have a seat at the table. We want to continue to sponsor more women to grow in corporate leadership.

Our Truths

Monica

Corporate America is in a state of emergency, and our call to action is to come together and work with policy change agents and really demand change. I keep saying the word "demand" because I think we have been talking about this for too long. I remember in the early 1980s and 1990s, when I was a child, my mother and aunt were talking about things like this. Now we're in 2022. We have to make it clear that racism and any kind of discrimination is unacceptable and that this cannot be okay in the workplace. Like Melody mentioned, most of the time it's the person who experienced this behavior who is reprimanded instead of the person who is the bad actor. They typically get to stay at the company and move up in the ranks and make upwards of $300,000 to $400,000 a year, if not more, with all sorts of annual bonuses and perks.

Melody

I think we are moving toward some change, but we have a ways to go. I would say that more women are speaking up about what they are experiencing. I remember people joking about how we got to go and deal with "the man." It's like this is what we know we have to deal with in order to provide for our family. These days, women and Black women specifically are demanding our worth. We know what we bring to the table. We see we are needed and we bring value, and now we can speak from a place of confidence instead of fearing for our job. It's now like if you don't see my value, treat me fairly, pay me fairly, I can leave and go somewhere else. More people are becoming entrepreneurs. Black women are the highest-rated group of entrepreneurs. They are tired of being devalued, tired of not being seen or heard, and we work 10-times faster and harder. There is no grace for us, so we are going to build our own companies.

With that being said, companies are trying to figure out how to retain these great employees because people are now just leaving. During the pandemic, more Black women resigned to pursue entrepreneurship. More Black women who were working from home quit their jobs because they didn't want to go back to the office and deal with microaggressions, racism, and a hostile work environment. The George Floyd and Breonna Taylor murders brought to the forefront racial tension we already knew existed. Racism was already happening but the tragedies are giving more people the voice to speak. The same way you see that white officer put his knee on that Black man's neck, this is how a lot of Black women have been feeling in the workplace. We are feeling like these white men, a white women, and other races have had their knees on our necks, and we are saying we can't deal with it. We are overwhelmed and something has to happen. People are finding their voices and are tired of the injustice. I would say the same injustices happening in the streets are happening in the workplace. In most cases it is subtle and appear as invisible. Because you're not seeing physical wounds, people take it lightly. It's like you don't know what we deal with when we go home. When we had our documentary screening, so many Black women felt safe because they realized they were not alone in this situation. This is another one of our reasons for making our story public, so Black women can feel like they have a safe haven and find the power within to tackle these issues.

Common Myths

COMMON MYTH:

Allies are not important in the fight against gender and race discrimination in the workplace.

TRUTH:

All voices need to be included, women and men. This is an inclusive call to action. We need some heads and real leaders, even if they are not Black, to be included in this. It needs to be understood that this is a universal problem.

The Real Truth

Monica

I think we as Black women do not help each other enough in the workplace. I back it up with that it's not by choice because even when a Black woman is in a management position or higher, many decisions are still not up to her. There is still someone else pulling the strings. Many times you receive batches of resumes and after you decide someone is a good fit, HR applies its filter and they bring in their referral or their friend's daughter or son. This makes it difficult for a Black woman in a management position, when the final say is not their own, to support other Black women.

The second part is, yes, it is our responsibility to help each other. I particularly talked to an HR professional who was a Black woman and her response to hiring people who look like her was that she needed to work with the white men or women and get them prepped to bring in a Black woman. I was just puzzled because even though you are in this head of a diversity role, you still don't have what it takes to bring in someone who looks like you. It is our responsibility because who else is going to do it? We know they will bring you in to be an individual contributor or to do the fine day-to-day tasks, but we are not talking about that. We are talking about being in decision-making roles and being on the board. We are talking about doing things that really show the skill set that we have and the contributions that we have been making for many years. So what does that look like when you get into a decision-making role? That means doing something as simple as working on benefits. I hate that we have to pitch that we need to hire more Black people, but that is where we are at. We need to meet them where they are and really express ourselves when we are in these roles. We do need to see more of us in these tech companies because it is inexcusable that we aren't present.

Melody

There are not enough Black women in leadership making decisions for women who are being underpaid or dealing with any type of racism or inequality in the workplace. There are not many decision-makers who can be advocates for us. In most organizations, there are numerous Black people in entry-level, customer service-type positions. Our fight is to get more Black executives so we can have someone to speak on our behalf. You can pull a seat up to the table but if you do not have a voice when you get there, it does not make any difference. Most of the time, you are the only one in the room. You do not have any power to make any change when it comes to it. Representation is key. When we think we have made it or we have accomplished getting into a specific high-level role, we do not want to cause any problems. There are stereotypes and many biases against Black women. We are called "the angry Black woman" or told we are being a bitch as we are too aggressive and hard to work with. All of these microaggressions effectively take a mental toll, which makes us always play it safe. This is true even if there is something that we know we can identify as wrong because as Black women we have experienced it so many times that we spot it very easily.

We still question ourselves: *"Is it us?"*

Usually, it is them, but we are so afraid to go off of our gut feeling because we do not want to cause trouble. We let the deck stack up against us and it harms us in the end in terms of our pay, as well as mentally, physically, and spiritually.

LET'S EXAMINE

ANALYZING GENDER AND RACE IN THE WORKPLACE

1. Addressing Equity

From February 2020 to January 2022, there were 2.6% less Black women in the workforce, the lowest number of any race and ethnic group in that timeframe.

Glynn, Sarah Jane, and Mark DeWolf. "Black Women's Economic Recovery Continues to Lag." United States Department of Labor, 9 Feb. 2022, blog.dol.gov.

Black women have a more difficult time at work compared to other races. According to Lean In's analysis of women in the workplace, the experience is worse for women than it is for men ("Women in the Workplace"). Women of color are experiencing worse conditions than white women, with Black women facing the most hardship. Many reasons contribute to the under-representation of Black women in the workplace. Stepping into higher management positions is one major factor. Despite requesting promotions at the same rate as men, only 58 Black women are promoted to manager for every 100 men ("The State of"). Black women are hired into manager roles at a rate of 64 per 100 men ("The State of"). The representation gap keeps widening as fewer Black women move up the ranks at every level. People often attribute Black women's achievements to factors beyond their control, factors such as affirmative action, helping others, or a lucky chance.

In other words, colleagues might say things like, *She only got the promotion because she was Black, and there is affirmative action.*

This thinking reinforces a damaging stereotype that depicts Black women as less capable and competent than their peers. Unchallenged, these comments may prevent Black women from receiving credit for their hard work and achievements. Management tends to provide less support and encouragement to women of color, and particularly Black women. The chances of Black women having managers showcase their work, advocate for new opportunities for them, or assign them work to manage people and projects are lower compared to white women ("The State of"). The proportion of Black women reporting that their managers help them cope with organizational politics or balance work and home life is also lower. In fact, consistently supportive managers are more likely to promote employees, and employees are more likely to believe they have equal opportunities for advancement.

Furthermore, women of color are significantly less likely to interact with senior leaders at work than their non-Black counterparts. In addition to diminished access, Black women are also lacking in sponsorship: Less than one-quarter of them have the support they need to advance their careers ("The State of"). Also, Black women have fewer opportunities to get noticed by people in leadership roles, and they are less likely to be included in important company conversations. The lack of an influential mentor was cited as a barrier to advancement by 62% of women of color with some level of mentorship and 30% of white men as well. Women at work are frequently subjected to microaggressions, which refer to comments and actions that subtly degrade or dismiss them because of their gender, race, or other characteristics of their identity. Because Black women face both racism and sexism, they encounter a greater number of microaggressions. They are more likely to be asked to provide additional evidence of their competence and to have their judgment questioned in their area of expertise. The likelihood of hearing someone in their workplace express surprise about their language skills or other abilities is more than three times greater for Black women than for white women.

2. The Balancing Act: Pay Equity vs. Performance

When a woman or a man asks for a raise, women are 25% less likely to receive it.

Crockett, Emily. "Women Negotiate for Raises as Much as Men Do. They Just Don't Get Them." *Vox*, 29 Sept. 2016, www.vox.com.

HR professionals should review their organization's compensation policies and practices as business leaders work to close the gender pay gap and states enact broader laws to ensure fair pay for more workers. By requiring employers to pay men and women equally for similar work instead of for equal work, many state laws provide broader protection than the federal Equal Pay Act. Furthermore, a number of states have extended the definition of fair pay to include race and other protected characteristics. What is pay equity? Employers are generally compensated the same no matter how similar their job duties are. It also implies taking other factors into consideration, such as an employee's experience level, performance on the job, and tenure with the company. Most state laws mandating greater transparency in the workplace and protecting employees from retaliation when they seek to correct wage disparities are in line with the Me Too movement. Employees may also be protected from retaliation when they discuss their pay openly with colleagues. Providing equal pay for employees can improve efficiency, creativity, and productivity by attracting the best employees, reducing turnover, and increasing employee commitment. Increasingly states are passing pay-equity laws, which has led to a dramatic rise in lawsuits against employers for equal pay and some multimillion-dollar settlements. For example, in 2019 Dell Technology agreed to settle claims alleging that it discriminated against women and minorities based on their race and gender ("U.S Department of Labor").

Performing an audit is a crucial step in identifying pay disparities and providing employers with ways to improve pay equity. Employers can determine if discrepancies are explicable by legitimate, nondiscriminatory reasons by conducting an audit. There are several legitimate business reasons for salary differences, including seniority, education, and job-specific experience. A thorough audit of a company's compensation program could also demonstrate areas where improvements may be made to prevent future unexplained pay disparities. A pay audit isn't just about determining whether there are pay disparities. It is also important for employers to understand why pay disparities exist. Economic experts work collaboratively to determine the right comparator groups, discuss pay practices, and provide all relevant pay data. They also can work together to identify and collect information regarding legitimate business factors that have an impact on compensation, as well as perform a proper statistical analysis to determine whether there are disparities based on gender or other protected categories. A deeper dive may require reviewing the documents and conducting interviews with decision-makers to determine whether appropriate comparator groups were used. Disparities should be documented when there are legitimate business reasons. It is often years after a pay decision that pay equity claims are asserted against employers. Pay equity should be kept in mind when HR develops workplace policies and procedures. The business should take into consideration how it determines starting pay, merit increases, promotions, raises, and incentives. Having salary controls in place during the recruitment process may prevent unexplained disparities. For example, an employer might offer a new hire a higher compensation package than existing employees in comparable positions in a tight labor market, which can result in an immediate pay gap.

3. Race, Ethnicity, and Other Key Considerations

Applicants with Black names are 10% less likely to get hired than applicants with a more white name.

Young, Robin, and Serena McMahon. "Name Discrimination Study Finds Lakisha and Jamal Still Less Likely to Get Hired than Emily and Greg." *WBUR*, 18 Aug. 2021, www.wbur.org.

Observing microaggressions as isolated incidents can make them seem insignificant. They build up and take a toll if they occur daily. It's disrespectful to insult people and invalidate them, whether it's intentional or unintentional. Being underestimated and slighted makes it hard for employees to deliver their best work. The number of women who regularly think about quitting their jobs increases threefold when they experience microaggressions ("The State of"). While Black women are no more likely than any other group of Americans to express anger, they often face racist remarks about how angry they are about the work treatment they receive. Almost half of Black women describe themselves as "Onlys," which means they are the only Black person or one of the only Black people in an important room at work. Women who are Onlys face special challenges. These individuals are very cognizant of the fact that they may be considered representatives of their race. They are more likely than members of other races and ethnicities to perceive their own failures and successes as reflecting on them. This makes them feel constantly on guard and under pressure to perform. Black women who are Onlys often feel like they are closely watched and are constantly on guard. White women and men perceive themselves to be allies to people of color at work more often than not. Almost a quarter of Black women think it is true that Black women have allies in the workplace, and less than half believe this is the case ("The State of"). Corporate America is dominated by white employees. In order to use their power effectively, they must establish allies and advocate for people of color. As allies, it's essential to speak out against racism in the workplace, yet only 40% of white employees have ever done so ("The State of"). The number of Black women considering becoming top executives is significantly higher than the number of white women. However, Black women are more likely to have a desire to positively influence the company culture or to be a role model for women like themselves. They know how difficult it can be to advance in a career as a woman of color, and they wish to make it easier for women like them.

We often perceive women as overly ambitious when they express the desire to lead because we expect them to be kind and motherly. Stereotypes can further compound this ambition penalty by portraying Black women as aggressive and angry. A majority of Black women aspiring to be top executives cite a desire to be role models for others as their motivation. Diversity efforts in corporations tend to be gender or race-oriented. Rarely do they focus on both. Women of color, who are confronted with sexism and racism more than any other group, are often overlooked. Specifically, companies need to address the barriers that prevent Black women from advancing, starting with letting everyone know why Black women's advancement is important to the company. A commitment must be made by companies to address the specific barriers that keep Black women from advancing. Diverse companies are more innovative and profitable. Their efforts are not only the right thing to do, it is the right thing for business too.

4. Measuring Pay Equity Gaps

Among Fortune 500 companies, only a little more than half release some data on their racial and ethnic makeup, with only 22 releasing full data.

Reiners, Bailey. "57 Diversity in the Workplace Statistics You Should Know." Edited by Hal Kloss, *Built In*, 21 Oct. 2021, builtin.com.

Since the Black Lives Matter and Me Too movements, pay equity has become a hot topic. As of March 2021, employers in California must submit equal pay reports annually. There have been a dozen states enacting or considering pay transparency legislation, including Colorado. Pay equity cannot be measured in a way that is universally applicable. There are topics of pay equity and gender pay gaps in some of the most recognized companies in our country. Investor activists, the C-suite, state and local government investigators, the Equal Employment Opportunity Commission, and class-action attorneys have all taken notice of this. As a result, many companies conduct proactive pay audits in an effort to quickly discover and remedy pay disparities. Some jurisdictions, in fact, will provide a complete defense to a claim under state law when such a self-audit is done before a lawsuit is filed. Audits of pay can be a very effective tool for achieving pay equity, provided they are conducted properly. Equal pay requires equal work under federal law. For comparable or substantially similar jobs, however, most states require equal pay. When the audit's main objective is limiting risk and making sure legal compliance is maintained with state and federal laws, identifying which employees perform comparable or substantially similar work will be a critical piece of the process. The obligation to pay employees equitably across lines of gender is also on the rise with the advent of new state equal pay laws. Race and nationality will also be protected. There are 13 protected classes in the Diane B. Allen Pay Equity Act in New Jersey, including race, gender, national origin, sexual orientation, and age.

Getting buy-in from senior management is another key to the planning process. Pay equity audits are extensive undertakings that require considerable resources. A company needs to formulate a budget that covers the costs associated with data collection and analysis, as well as correcting possible pay disparities. As part of the audit process, it is important to take the time to examine or re-examine historical and current pay practices and policies to establish the correct methodology for analyzing pay and to understand and explain pay disparities. In order to make effective compensation decisions, it is essential to understand the factors that determine compensation, how decision-makers make pay decisions, and how much discretion individuals have when it comes to making compensation decisions. Experience has shown answers to these questions often differ within an organization by department or geography, particularly when the business has grown through acquisitions.

Gather the relevant data to analyze pay after examining the components of pay and the criteria for determining pay. Accordingly, the data for each employee involved in the analysis typically includes title, department, hire date, gender, and any other protected group identifiers such as race, location, salary, overtime, bonuses, and other forms of compensation for the previous 52 weeks. In addition to performance scores and/or ratings, it may be vital to collect information such as education level and experience in the relevant field or industry based on the criteria for making pay decisions within your company or department.

5. Closing Pay Equity Gap

In 1980, women between 25 and 34 made 33 cents less than men, compared to 7 cents in 2020.

Barroso, Amanda, and Anna Brown. "Gender Pay Gap in U.S. Held Steady in 2020." *Pew Research Center*, 25 May 2021, www.pewresearch.org.

Often payroll databases do not capture all of the information necessary to make pay decisions, making comprehensive pay audits difficult for employers. Data collection can be very labor- and time-intensive in such situations. State law defines "comparable" or "substantially similar" work more broadly and inclusively than federal law defines "equal work." It is typically defined as work that is similar in terms of skills, responsibilities, and effort, as well as the conditions under which the work is done. Examining a job as a whole is necessary to determine whether it is equivalent. Even though job titles and descriptions can be useful, comparing them alone should not be the determining factor. Additionally, do not assume that jobs within different departments or business units cannot be compared. The difference in skills, responsibilities, and effort between the two jobs, as well as working conditions, should be examined. Additionally, you should consider any state-specific requirements or guidance for grouping employees based on the state(s) in which individuals work. Once the employees are broken into comparable job groups, analyze the data, paying equal attention to men and women (or other protected classes). Based on the group size and the complexity of the compensation program, the methodology can differ. The most reliable way to identify potentially unlawful disparities is to use regression analysis that controls for variables such as length of time on the job, years of experience, or performance ratings. Take steps to remedy the pay disparity where one or more legal reasons cannot be cited for the differential. Your company may need to adjust compensation in most cases. Pay disparities cannot be remedied by reducing the salaries of employees. In addition, when making adjustments to pay, consider the timing and, whenever possible, include them in annual pay adjustments. In addition, it is crucial that the pay audit findings are communicated to hiring managers and others responsible for pay decisions. By addressing these issues, inequities will not be perpetuated.

Closing the pay gap is crucial to creating economic equality, but for many reasons and laws, it still remains an elusive goal. One contributing issue is that talking openly about employee compensation is considered taboo in the workplace. This results in people not understanding the kind of pay they deserve or should expect to receive. Pay equity must be enforced within organizations by human resources departments to advance the goal of closing the pay gap. As stated, in order to determine the pay rates within your organization, you must conduct a pay equity audit or equal pay audit. A variety of factors are considered when assessing pay based on age, race, gender, job description and responsibilities, and seniority. Pay equity analyses insulate the company against wage discrimination lawsuits. The wage gap is drawing more attention than ever from state and federal governments, media outlets, and judicial bodies.

6. Let's Talk About Systemic Equity

78% of black people believe the country has not gone far enough to help Blacks have equal rights to whites.

Horowitz, Juliana Menasce, et al. "Race in America 2019." *Pew Research Center*, 9 Apr. 2019, www.pewresearch.org.

The systemic inequity in the workplace is comparable to what occurs in U.S classrooms. The root cause of many issues that people of color face in their adult lives can in fact be traced back to racism in education (Chatterji). Every person experiences systemic change differently. Most efforts to transform systems fail because of this simple but paradoxical idea. There is something in the word "system" or "systemic" that consistently causes us to misunderstand. Nowhere is this misconception more tragic than in efforts to address the inequity in the American school system. The many tangible aspects of educational inequity, including class size, teacher preparation, curricular relevance, and student opportunity, are inextricably linked to students' abilities and potential. With the right information, incentives, and investments, racism in the workplace can be effectively addressed. It may not be possible for corporate leaders to change the world, but it is certainly possible for them to change their own business culture and practices. A relatively small, autonomous organization's cultural norms and procedural rules can be highly controlled by its leaders. Therefore, they are ideal places for promoting racial equity policies. Organizations must resist the urge to seek immediate relief for systemic equity symptoms and instead focus on the overall disease.

To effectively address racism in your organization, it's important to build consensus around whether there is a problem, then identify what it is and the root cause. If any employees do not believe racism against people of color exists in the organization, then diversity initiatives will be perceived as the problem, not the solution. Due to this, mid-level managers often resist such initiatives with resentment. The outcome of efforts to increase equity is determined by employees' beliefs. Getting everyone on the same page about the reality of the situation and why it's a problem is the first step. It may seem obvious that racism continues to oppress people of color, yet research consistently reveals many white people don't see it that way. Based on a 2011 study by Michael Norton and Sam Sommers, whites in the United States believe that systemic racism against Blacks has steadily decreased and systemic racism against whites has increased. As a whole, whites believe there is more racism against them than against Black people. Moreover, 66% of working-class whites consider discrimination against them to be as big of a problem as discrimination against people of color. These beliefs are critical because they can undermine the company's goal to combat racism by lessening support for diversity policies. Some managers who can recognize racism in overall society often fail to see it in their own business. Some executives point to their commitment to inclusion and diversity as evidence of the absence of any racial discrimination.

Research has documented that racial discrimination is prevalent in the workplace and even with strong commitments to expanding diversity, the company can likely still discriminate. Some white people deny the existence of racism because they assume racism is defined by deliberate actions motivated by true hatred. They need to understand that racism can occur without awareness or intent. When defined simply as differential treatment based on race regardless of intent, racism occurs in the workplace far more frequently than most white people realize.

7. The Next Generation of Gap Closers

As of 2021, 39.1% of US women have a four-year college degree.

Duffin, Erin. "Percentage of the U.S. Population who have Completed Four Years of College or More from 1940 to 2021, by Gender." *Statista*, 27 July 2022, www.statista.com.

According to a 2019 article from the Society for Human Resource Management, the educational and career choices women make fueled by the "opportunity gap" or barriers that prevent women from pursuing higher paying careers could be responsible for the gender pay gap (Miller). Historically, people have viewed Black women as less deserving than our white and other counterparts. This is due to the bias and systemic barriers we faced with daily. Some have pointed out that women do not earn as much as men due to their commitment to family responsibilities throughout their careers. According to a study published on Statista analyzing the college graduate outcomes of hundreds of thousands of 2020 class members, women earned $52,266 on average while men earned $64,022 on average (Duffin). The data also showed that the field of study did not fully explain why men consistently earn more than women. The 2022 Equal Pay Day was Tuesday, March 15. This date marks how far into the year women must work to earn what men earned in the previous year. Equal Pay Day, previously known as National Pay Inequity Awareness Day, was established in 1996 to shine a light on the pay gap between men and women. Women who work full time and year round make 17% less than men ("Women are Paid"). Among all workers, including the millions of people who worked part-time because of COVID-19, the gender pay gap is a shocking 27% ("Women are Paid"). Women graduate from college at a higher rate than men, and this has been the case for the last few decades ("Women are Paid"). Diplomas do not automatically equal higher salaries. The pay gap remains for employees with higher education levels and actually has increased for some women in the workforce. Additionally, research shows when women join an industry in large numbers, the pay rate goes down. The pay gap is not just a paycheck. Add this up over the course of a career and the lost income can be millions of dollars. Typically, young people with college degrees are now earning more than their high-school-graduate peers by $22,000 per year. An annual wage of $30,000 is the median wage for a full-time worker with a high school diploma ages 22 to 27 (Schaeffer).

This huge difference in pay is the highest on record. The New York Federal Commission researched earnings by major for recent and for mid-career college graduates. Recent graduates are categorized between 22 and 27 years of age, and mid-career graduates are 35 and 45 years of age. For both recent and mid-career graduates, engineering and STEM majors were the top-earning positions.

Highest-paying majors for recent graduates:

- Computer engineering: $74,000
- Chemical engineering: $70,000
- Aerospace engineering: $70,000
- Electrical engineering: $70,000
- Computer science: $70,000

Highest-paying majors for mid-career graduates:

- Chemical engineering: $111,000
- Computer engineering: $110,000
- Aerospace engineering: $110,000
- Electrical engineering: $107,000
- Mechanical engineering: $104,000

Lowest-paying majors for recent graduates:

- Family and consumer sciences: $32,000
- General social sciences: $34,000
- Performing arts: $34,000
- Social services: $35,000
- Anthropology: $36,000

Lowest-paying majors for mid-career graduates:

- Early childhood education: $43,700
- Elementary education: $45,400
- Social services: $50,000
- General education: $50,000
- Family and consumer sciences: $51,000

Caveats:

Monica

There is something very concerning that is happening within the Black community in terms of women being fairly paid. Black women's Equal Pay Day for 2022 was pushed out an entire month showing that Covid-19 has widened the pay gap for Black women ("This Equal"). When we speak within corporations on change and diversity, we have to speak to how we are going to make the corporation's space equitable. We are not only trying to fix years of Black women being underpaid, but now we are also trying to fix what happened in 2020. Where do we start? How can we start? How can these companies bring a collaborative environment and make sure that they are being transparent in terms of roles and pay? There should never be a question if you are making the same amount of money as a coworker who does the same job and has the same experience. It is so important that we address how Covid-19 impacted the wage gap by making it even wider for Black women.

Melody

Ultimately, as Black women, we cannot wait. According to the World Economic Forum's Global Gender Gap report from 2022, the pay gap is estimated to close in 132 years (Kali Pal). I won't even be alive then, so as Black women, we cannot wait. There is already a large gap that Black women are facing, and we have many responsibilities to fulfill that are impacted by that gap. We are the heads of our households and breadwinners. It trickles down for generations and as much work as Black women have put into building America, we deserve to be able to live a good life financially. We deserve to have access to wealth. We need people to rally together, stand up, and take this seriously. A lot of times people truly don't understand it. They feel that you get paid what you do and that it's working, but we really are behind. We have got to keep working at it

Commentary

Monica

This is a state of emergency, and we need to talk about the state of Black women in the workplace immediately. We have to come up with viable solutions. Black women are tired of talking because we've done enough of it. Our mouths are dry. We are tired of acting and we are tired of begging. It is now the time for immediate solutions.

If someone disagrees with the fact that Black women are underpaid and facing racism on the job, I would ask for case studies that support their thinking. . There are very few studies that show the opposite of what we've been discussing and it can be shown through how the workplace impacts a Black woman's personal life. If you are being underpaid at work and struggling to make ends meet, now you have to deal with your husband and kids. Nevermind the fact that Black men are underpaid as well, now we are dealing with a home that is barely making it. We know that when you don't have enough and when you can't make ends meet, there is an air of frustration. There is no happiness at work or at home for the Black woman if we continue at the rate that we are being underpaid.

Melody

We can't wait anymore. Black women are working quicker, faster, harder, and many Black women have to work two to three jobs in order to get by. We should be able to have a life where we can reap the benefits of the work that we are doing for our families, communities, and for these companies. We are making everybody rich and wealthy but ourselves. Over a lifespan, we are losing out on so much money. When you look at it hourly, it doesn't sound as bad but over time, we are missing out. That is money that we could be investing or buying homes with. We are demanding that we get what we are worth right now.

The pay gap that exists for Black women is not a myth. It is a fact. There is a good amount of data and reports, some of which we've included in this book, that validate the pay gap. How Black women are paid and treated in the workplace also aligns with how Black women appear in the media, which is undervalued. There is a dollar amount that is associated with being valued and Black women are undervalued. I guarantee that as a Black woman, even the top executives, you have been underpaid or under appreciated at some point in your career. You have to realize your own value.

CASE STUDY

SHANNON POWER, VP OF FINANCE

1. HAS A COMPANY YOU CURRENTLY WORK FOR, PREVIOUSLY WORKED FOR, OR OWNED EVER DONE A PAY AUDIT?

I have not worked at a company that has done a pay audit. While I do feel like it can be a good starting place for unfair wage practices, I don't feel that it is the end-all-be-all by any means. It is a piece of it. You can do a one-time pay audit, realize there are some discrepancies, and then adjust those that were unfairly lower. But what is not always done, and I think is even more important, is to also teach. We need to teach negotiation skills, teach people how to be advocates for themselves, women, and people of color. We are not given those tools and white men traditionally have more experience in asking for what they want. The social conditioning that women experience, to sit looking pretty and wait to be asked, needs to change. We need to teach women how to advocate and negotiate for themselves, otherwise a pay audit will result in a one-time bump and that's it. The gap continues unless you teach people, specifically women and people of color, how to advocate for themselves for wage increases, promotion availability, and promotions. Audits can be a good starting place for companies, however, I feel that the constant advocacy, negotiation skill building, and the practice of asking for what you want is an even more effective tool to continue.

2. ARE THERE OTHER POLICIES OR PROCEDURES THAT YOU FEEL COULD EFFECTIVELY LIMIT THE WAGE GAP?

I think a big factor is that we need more women and people of color in leadership positions. It's very hard for most people to believe that they can be in those roles unless they see someone they identify with in that role as well. My passion is advocating for gender equality in corporate leadership. The world and the workplace would be better places if we had more women leaders.

3. HAVE YOU STRUGGLED OR SEEN COWORKERS STRUGGLING TO FIND BLACK FEMALE MENTORS AND LEADERS IN THE WORKPLACE?

Yes, absolutely. There are not enough Black women within corporate leadership in America. I feel that it is also an ally's job to help lift as we rise, to advocate for consciously and intentionally diversifying our teams. Providing opportunities and promotions to Black women is so important in ensuring that they are equally represented in leadership positions.

4. WHAT IS YOUR CURRENT OCCUPATION? WHAT WAS YOUR JOURNEY LIKE TO GETTING TO WHERE YOU ARE NOW, AND WHEN DID YOU FIRST RECOGNIZE THE GENDER PAY GAP IN YOUR PROFESSIONAL EXPERIENCES?

I am the vice president of finance of a multi-billion dollar software company. My first experience with the gender pay gap didn't come until later on in my career. I was reviewing my departments' budget with my financial analyst. My financial analyst was flipping across departments' spreadsheets and trying to filter out just the cost center for my departments. She was sharing her entire screen and happened to show another department's cost center. I saw that a colleague of mine, who happens to be male and white, was being paid quite a bit more than I was. I was shocked and I felt offended. After finding out I did some soul searching, went on a long run, and tried to figure out what I should do about it. At that point in time, I was being considered for a promotion. When I soul searched and thought about my career and personal goals, I actually decided not to do anything. Truth be told, within three months I was promoted and after the promotion I felt well compensated.

Let's Discuss

1. Can the workplace ever be equal?

_____

_____

_____

_____

_____

_____

_____

_____

_____

_____

_____

_____

_____

Let's Discuss

2. Does race/sex play a role in the hiring process?

_____

_____

_____

_____

_____

_____

_____

_____

_____

_____

_____

Let's Discuss

3. Are there enough Black women in leadership?

_____

_____

_____

_____

_____

_____

_____

_____

_____

_____

_____

_____

_____

Let's Discuss

4. Should men be in the movement?

_____

_____

_____

_____

_____

_____

_____

_____

_____

_____

_____

_____

Let's Discuss

5. Have women made progress in the workplace over the last four decades?

_____

_____

_____

_____

_____

_____

_____

_____

_____

_____

_____

_____

Let's Discuss

6. Is the movement for change strong enough?

_____

_____

_____

_____

_____

_____

_____

_____

_____

_____

_____

_____

_____

Let's Discuss

7. Do men understand the remote workplace struggle?

_____

_____

_____

_____

_____

_____

_____

_____

_____

_____

_____

_____

_____

Let's Discuss

8. Is there a promise for the next generation?

_____

_____

_____

_____

_____

_____

_____

_____

_____

_____

_____

_____

Let's Discuss

9.   Who holds power in the workplace?

_____

_____

_____

_____

_____

_____

_____

_____

_____

_____

_____

_____

Let's Discuss

10. Is BLM and the Women's Rights Movement united or independent entities?

_____

_____

_____

_____

_____

_____

_____

_____

_____

_____

_____

_____

Let's Discuss

11. Is corporate work built off the patriarchy?

_____

_____

_____

_____

_____

_____

_____

_____

_____

_____

_____

_____

_____

Let's Discuss

12. Do you, as a woman, feel an extra layer of stress at work?

_____

_____

_____

_____

_____

_____

_____

_____

_____

_____

_____

_____

Let's Discuss

13. Do you feel your employer cares more about you or profits?

_____

_____

_____

_____

_____

_____

_____

_____

_____

_____

_____

_____

Prompts with Purpose

1. Write down your current pay. Do you feel that you are paid fairly in comparison to your coworkers? How about in comparison to the amount of effort you put in?

_____

_____

_____

_____

_____

_____

_____

_____

_____

_____

_____

_____

Prompts with Purpose

2. Do you feel safe in your workplace?

_____

_____

_____

_____

_____

_____

_____

_____

_____

_____

_____

_____

_____

Prompts with Purpose

3. Our experiences, good and bad, can shape the way
    we feel and act. This applies to the workplace as well.
    Though the bad may impact us negatively, we can also
    grow from it. What are some ways that you excel at your
    job because of your experiences?

_____

_____

_____

_____

_____

_____

_____

_____

_____

_____

_____

THE INVISIBLE WOMAN'S
AFFIRMATION

I HOLD POWER. MY LIMITS ARE
NOT DEFINED BY OTHERS.

EPILOGUE

The introduction of the Me Too movement began a long needed discussion on sexism in the workplace, but the inequities that Black women faced were still plaguing every professional setting with significantly less public out-cry. Black women face workplace discrimination everyday at alarming rates. Throughout this book, we have explored gender and race discrimination in the workplace through qauntitative and qualitative studies as well as through our personal experiences all to showcase not only the issues, but the possible solutions. Black women's power and presence in the workplace is irreplace-able. Our power is the all-too-often unrecognized glue that holds the team together and hands that mold the project. It is time we are seen that way.

Our lives have not always been easy. We began our careers and experienced multiple kinds of discrimination in many types of environments. Our climb to the top came out of our personal necessity to see Black women in import-ant positions. Positions most often given to white men. Our hope is that our stories can be starting points for the next generation to begin advocating for themselves and their peers. We hope that this book will be a resource in your journey to your own professional empowerment.

21 DAYS OF EMPOWERMENT

Day 1

1. Write about your professional journey. How did you get to where you are now? Take a moment to reflect, no matter where you are in life, on how far you have come. You have worked hard. Allow yourself to recognize that effort.

_____

_____

_____

_____

_____

_____

_____

_____

_____

_____

_____

_____

_____

Day 2

2. Make a list of your top five short-term and top five long-term goals. With each goal, write down what steps you are currently taking and what steps you will take in the future to accomplish that goal.

_____

_____

_____

_____

_____

_____

_____

_____

_____

_____

_____

_____

Day 3

3. What are your greatest professional strengths? How do you utilize those strengths every day? Weekly? Yearly?

_____

_____

_____

_____

_____

_____

_____

_____

_____

_____

_____

_____

Day 4

4. What are your greatest professional weaknesses? What steps are you taking to improve upon them?

_____

_____

_____

_____

_____

_____

_____

_____

_____

_____

_____

_____

Day 5

5. What is an area in your career that you wish to strengthen? How can you work to do so on a daily basis?

_____

_____

_____

_____

_____

_____

_____

_____

_____

_____

_____

_____

Day 6

6. Do you feel fulfilled by your current career choice? Why or why not?

_____

_____

_____

_____

_____

_____

_____

_____

_____

_____

_____

_____

Day 7

7. Realistically, where do you see yourself in one year? How about five years? Does your current path match your long-term goals?

_____

_____

_____

_____

_____

_____

_____

_____

_____

_____

_____

_____

Day 8

8. What do you enjoy most about your job? How can you incorporate that joy into your daily routine?

_____

_____

_____

_____

_____

_____

_____

_____

_____

_____

_____

_____

Day 9

9. What is a mistake you've made in your career that has impacted the way you work today? How have you learned or can you learn from it?

_____

_____

_____

_____

_____

_____

_____

_____

_____

_____

_____

_____

Day 10

10. What is your proudest professional accomplishment?

_____

_____

_____

_____

_____

_____

_____

_____

_____

_____

_____

_____

Day 11

11. Do you feel like you have a good work-life balance? What are ways you can or have set up boundaries in your professional life?

_____

_____

_____

_____

_____

_____

_____

_____

_____

_____

_____

_____

Day 12

12. Who is your role model? Why? How does their influence impact your professional and personal life?

_____

_____

_____

_____

_____

_____

_____

_____

_____

_____

_____

_____

Day 13

13. Have you ever lost out on a promotion or lost a job? Allow yourself a moment to reflect on how that made you feel.

_____

_____

_____

_____

_____

_____

_____

_____

_____

_____

_____

_____

_____

Day 14

14. What are you most grateful for in your professional life? Your personal life? How does that gratitude manifest in your everyday life?

_____

_____

_____

_____

_____

_____

_____

_____

_____

_____

_____

_____

Day 15

15. How do you feel at the end of each work week? If you are feeling burned out, what actions can you take during the work week to make you feel less overwhelmed?

_____

_____

_____

_____

_____

_____

_____

_____

_____

_____

_____

_____

Day 16

16. What is your greatest challenge at work? What steps can you take to either overcome that challenge or become better prepared to face it?

_____

_____

_____

_____

_____

_____

_____

_____

_____

_____

_____

_____

Day 17

17. In your current profession, what would you define as success? Is that something you'd like to achieve? If yes, what are the steps you can take to reach that goal? If no, what is stopping you from transitioning to another profession?

Day 18

18. What are the things that make you feel most empowered? How can you incorporate them into your daily life?

_____

_____

_____

_____

_____

_____

_____

_____

_____

_____

_____

_____

Day 19

19. What are your favorite stress-relieving activities? Is there a way you can bring them into your daily routine?

_____

_____

_____

_____

_____

_____

_____

_____

_____

_____

_____

_____

_____

Day 20

20. How do you advocate for yourself in your profession? If you don't, what are steps you can take to do so?

_____

_____

_____

_____

_____

_____

_____

_____

_____

_____

_____

_____

Day 21

21. Make a list of how you bring value to your work and personal life. Be proud of yourself. You deserve it.

_____

_____

_____

_____

_____

_____

_____

_____

_____

_____

_____

_____

_____

PLAYLIST

1. Rise Up - Andra Day

2. Independent Women, Pt. 1 - Destiny's Child

3. Confident - Demi Lovato

4. Run the World (Girls) - Beyoncé

5. Good as Hell - Lizzo

6. Respect - Aretha Franklin

7. Girl On Fire - Alicia Keys

8. ***Flawless (Feat. Chimamanda Ngozi Adichie) - Beyoncé

9. Unstoppable - Sia

10. I Will Survive - Gloria Gaynor

11. Break My Soul - Beyoncé

12. Her - Megan Thee Stallion

13. Woman Like Me (Feat. Nicki Minaj) - Little Mix

14. The Edge of Glory - Lady Gaga

15. Savage Remix (Feat. Beyoncé) - Megan Thee Stallion

16.   We Run This - Missy Elliot

17.   I'm Every Woman - Chaka Khan

18.   Brave - Sara Bareilles

19.   About Damn Time - Lizzo

20.   7 Rings - Ariana Grande

BIBLIOGRAPHY

PART I:

Bialik, Kristen, et al. "Strong Men, Caring Women: How Americans Describe What Society Values (and Doesn't) in Each Gender." *Pew Research Center's Social & Demographic Trends Project*, Pew Research Center, 24 July 2018, https://www.pewresearch.org/social-trends/interactives/strong-men-caring-women/.

Canon, Maria E., et al. "Understanding the Gender Earnings Gap: Hours Worked, Occupational Sorting, and Labor Market Experience." *Economic Research - Federal Reserve Bank of St. Louis*, 2021, https://research.stlouisfed.org/publications/review/2021/04/15/understanding-the-gender-earnings-gap-hours-worked-occupational-sorting-and-labor-market-experience.

"Equal Pay Act." *History.com*, A&E Television Networks, 2 Apr. 2019, https://www.history.com/topics/womens-rights/equal-pay-act.

"Equal Pay for Work of Equal Value." *UN Women*, 2017, https://www.unwomen.org/en/news/in-focus/csw61/equal-pay.

Fry, Richard. "Some Gender Disparities Widened in the U.S. Workforce During the Pandemic." *Pew Research Center*, Pew Research Center, 14 Jan. 2022, https://www.pewresearch.org/fact-tank/2022/01/14/

some-gender-disparities-widened-in-the-u-s-workforce-during-the-pandemic/.

Gilchrist, Karen. "Men Are Not the Only Ones Biased against Women, UN Study Finds." *CNBC*, CNBC, 6 Mar. 2020, https://www.cnbc.com/2020/03/06/united-nations-almost-90percent-of-people-are-biased-against-women.html.

Iacurci, Greg. "Women Are Still Paid 83 Cents for Every Dollar Men Earn. Here's Why." *CNBC*, 19 May 2022, https://www.cnbc.com/2022/05/19/women-are-still-paid-83-cents-for-every-dollar-men-earn-heres-why.html.

Jones, Martha S. "What the 19th Amendment Meant for Black Women." *POLITICO*, 6 Aug. 2020, https://www.politico.com/news/magazine/2020/08/26/19th-amendment-meant-for-black-women-400995.

"Know Your Rights at Work: Pay Discrimination." *Equal Rights Advocates*, 18 Aug. 2022, https://www.equalrights.org/issue/economic-workplace-equality/pay-discrimination/#:~:text=Title%20VII%20of%20the%20Civil,%2C%20religion%2C%20or%20national%20or-igin.

Miller, Stephen. "Gender Pay Gap Improvement Slowed During the Pandemic." *SHRM*, SHRM, 15 Mar. 2022, https://www.shrm.org/resourcesandtools/hr-topics/compensation/pages/gender-pay-gap-improvement-slowed-during-the-pandemic.aspx.

Perry, Mark J. "There Really Is No 'Gender Wage Gap.' There's a 'Gender Earnings Gap...'" *AEI*, 31 July 2017, https://www.aei.org/carpe-diem/there-really-is-no-gender-wage-gap-there-is-a-gender-earnings-gap-but-paying-women-well-wont-close-that-gap/.

Pinkus, Erin. "LeanIn.org: Surveymonkey Poll: Equal Pay Day 2021." *SurveyMonkey*, 2021, https://www.surveymonkey.com/curiosity/lean-in-poll-equal-pay-day-2021/.

Qureshi, Lyla. "Dissecting C-Suite Gender Pay Disparity." *The Harvard Law School Forum on Corporate Governance*, 1

Aug. 2018, https://corpgov.law.harvard.edu/2018/08/01/dissecting-c-suite-gender-pay-disparity/.

Smith, Morgan. "These 5 Industries Have the Biggest Gender Pay Gaps–Here's Why." *CNBC*, 30 Mar. 2022,

"The System Is Failing Latinas and Black Women." *Lean In*, 2021, https://leanin.org/research/equal-pay-day-2021.

"Tackling The Gender Pay Gap - UN Women." *UN Women*, 2016, https://www.unwomen.org/sites/default/files/Headquarters/Attachments/Sections/Library/Publications/2016/UN-Women-Policy-brief-06-Tackling-the-gender-pay-gap-en.pdf.

PART II:

Ariella, Sky. "25 Women in Leadership Statistics [2022]: Facts on the Gender Gap in Corporate and Political Leadership." *Zippia 25 Women In Leadership Statistics 2022 Facts On The Gender Gap In Corporate And Political Leadership Comments*, Zippia, 19 Apr. 2022, https://www.zippia.com/advice/women-in-leadership-statistics/.

Browley, Jasmine. "Report: Black Professionals Leaving the Workforce to Become Entrepreneurs." *Essence*, 15 Feb. 2022, https://www.essence.com/news/black-professionals-leaving-workforce-to-become-entrepr-eneurs/.

"California SB 1162." *Open States*, Civic Eagle, 2022, https://openstates.org/ca/bills/20212022/SB1162/.

"11 Surprising Job Satisfaction Statistics (2022)." *Apollo Technical LLC*, 14 Feb. 2022, https://www.apollotechnical.com/job-satisfaction-statistics/.

Ellingrud, Kweilin. "What We Lose When We Lose Women in the Workforce." *McKinsey & Company*, 3 June 2021, https://www.mckinsey.com/featured-insights/

sustainable-inclusive-growth/future-of-america/
what-we-lose-when-we-lose-women-in-the-workforce.

"Employment Characteristics of Families–2021." *U.S. Bureau of Labor Statistics*, 20 Apr. 2022, https://www.bls.gov/news.release/pdf/famee.pdf.

Heggeness, Misty L, et al. "Tracking Job Losses for Mothers of School-Age Children during a Health Crisis." *United States Census Bureau*, 3 Mar. 2021, https://www.census.gov/library/stories/2021/03/moms-work-and-the-pandemic.html.

Hewlett, Sylvia Ann, et al. "Diversity Joint Venture for Careers in Conservation, 2017." *Easing Racial Tensions*, https://diversityinconservationjobs.org/wp-content/uploads/2018/09/EasingRacialTensionsAtWork_Report-June2017-CTI.pdf.

Hewlett, Sylvia Ann, et al. 5th ed., INSEAD, Fontainebleau, France, 2018, pp. 45–51, *The Global Talent Competitiveness Index 2018*, https://www.insead.edu/sites/default/files/assets/dept/globalindices/docs/GTCI-2018-report.pdf.

Ibarra, Herminia, et al. "Why Men Still Get More Promotions Than Women." *Harvard Business Review*, Harvard Business School Publishing, Sept. 2010, https://hbr.org/2010/09/why-men-still-get-more-promotions-than-women.

Kennedy, Julia Taylor, et al. "The Power of Belonging and Why It Matters in Today's Workplace." *Coqual*, ServiceNow, 2020, https://coqual.org/wp-content/uploads/2020/09/CoqualPowerOfBelongingKeyFindings090720.pdf.

Lee, Nathaniel. "Why American Wages Haven't Grown Despite Increases in Productivity." *CNBC*, 19 July 2022, https://www.cnbc.com/2022/07/19/heres-how-labor-dynamism-affects-wage-growth-in-america.html#:~:text=Wages%20in%20the%20U.S.%20have,fellow%20at%20the%20Manhattan%20Institute.

McCarthy, Joe. "What Is the Gender Pay Gap and How Do We Close It?" *Global Citizen*, Global Poverty Project, Inc, 11 Mar. 2021, https://www.globalcitizen.org/en/content/what-is-the-gender-pay-gap/.

Parker, Kim, and Juliana Menasce Horowitz. "Majority of Workers Who Quit a Job in 2021 Cite Low Pay, No Opportunities for Advancement, Feeling Disrespected." *Pew Research Center*, 9 Mar. 2022, https://www.pewresearch.org/fact-tank/2022/03/09/majority-of-workers-who-quit-a-job-in-2021-cite-low-pay-no-opportunities-for-advancement-feeling-disrespected/.

Peakman, Vicky. "Break the Bias: Celebrating International Women's Day by Examining What Drives Pay Gaps." *Payscale*, 7 Mar. 2022, https://www.payscale.com/compensation-trends/break-the-bias-celebrating-international-womens-day-by-examining-what-drives-pay-gaps/.

"The Simple Truth About the Gender Pay Gap: AAUW Report." *AAUW*, 2021, https://www.aauw.org/resources/research/simple-truth/.

Smith, Morgan. "These 5 Industries Have the Biggest Gender Pay Gaps--Here's Why." *CNBC*, 30 Mar. 2022, https://www.cnbc.com/2022/03/30/these-5-industries-have-the-biggest-gender-pay-gapsheres-why-.html.

Thomas, Patrick. "Google Settles Gender Discrimination Lawsuit for $118 Million." *The Wall Street Journal*, Dow Jones & Company, 12 June 2022, https://www.wsj.com/articles/google-settles-gender-discrimination-lawsuit-for-118-million-11655079036.

Wheelwright, Trevor. "The Gender Pay Gap across the US in 2022." *Business.org*, 1 Mar. 2022, https://www.business.org/hr/benefits/gender-pay-gap/.

White, Gillian B. "Black Workers Really Do Need to Be Twice as Good." *The Atlantic*, Atlantic Media Company, 7 Oct. 2015, https://www.theatlantic.com/business/archive/2015/10/why-black-workers-really-do-need-to-be-twice-as-good/409276/.

"Women in Male-Dominated Industries and Occupations (Quick Take)." *Catalyst*, 21 Jan. 2022, https://www.catalyst.org/

research/women-in-male-dominated-industries-and-occupations/#:~:text=Male%2Ddominated%20industries%20and%20occupations%20are%20particularly%20vulnerable%20to%20reinforcing,male%2Ddominated%20occupations%20in%202020

"Women in the Workplace 2021." *Lean In*, 2021, https://leanin.org/women-in-the-workplace-report-2021/how-companies-can-advance-diversity-and-inclusion.

"Women More Likely than Men to Have Earned a Bachelor's Degree by Age 31." *The Economics Daily*, U.S. Bureau of Labor Statistics, 6 Dec. 2018, https://www.bls.gov/opub/ted/2018/women-more-likely-than-men-to-have-earned-a-bachelors-degree-by-age-31.htm.

"Women Much More Likely than Men to Give up Paid Work or Cut Hours after Childbirth Even When They Earn More." *IFS*, 12 Mar. 2021, https://ifs.org.uk/publications/15359.

Worthy, Patrice. "Black Women Say Goodbye to the Job and Hello to Their Own Businesses." *The Guardian*, Guardian News and Media, 12 Feb. 2022, https://www.theguardian.com/business/2022/feb/12/black-women-say-goodbye-to-the-job-and-hello-to-their-own-businesses.

Zheng, Lily. "Do Your Employees Feel Safe Reporting Abuse and Discrimination?" *Harvard Business Review*, Harvard Business School Publishing, 8 Oct. 2020, https://hbr.org/2020/10/do-your-employees-feel-safe-reporting-abuse-and-discrimination.

PART III:

Barroso, Amanda, and Anna Brown. "Gender Pay Gap in U.S. Held Steady in 2020." *Pew Research Center*, 25 May 2021, https://www.pewresearch.org/fact-tank/2021/05/25/gender-pay-gap-facts/.

Brooks, Khristopher J. "Why so Many Black Business Professionals Are Missing from the C-Suite." *CBS News*, CBS Interactive, 10 Dec. 2019, https://www.cbsnews.com/news/

black-professionals-hold-only-3-percent-of-executive-jobs-1-percent-of-ceo-jobs-at-fortune-500-firms-new-report-says/.

Chatterji, Roby. "Fighting Systemic Racism in K-12 Education: Helping Allies Move from the Keyboard to the School Board." *Center for American Progress*, 8 July 2020, https://www.americanprogress.org/article/fighting-systemic-racism-k-12-education-helping-allies-move-keyboard-school-board/.

Crockett, Emily. "Women Negotiate for Raises as Much as Men Do. They Just Don't Get Them." *Vox*, 29 Sept. 2016, https://www.vox.com/identities/2016/9/29/13096310/wage-gap-women-negotiate-lean-in.

Duffin, Erin. "Percentage of the U.S. Population who have Completed Four Years of College or More from 1940 to 2021, by Gender." *Statista*, 27 July 2022, https://www.statista.com/statistics/184272/educational-attainment-of-college-diploma-or-higher-by-gender/.

Glynn, Sarah Jane, and Mark DeWolf. "Black Women's Economic Recovery Continues to Lag." *United States Department of Labor*, 9 Feb. 2022, https://blog.dol.gov/2022/02/09/black-womens-economic-recovery-continues-to-lag.

Horowitz, Juliana Menasce, et al. "Race in America 2019." *Pew Research Center*, 9 Apr. 2019, https://www.pewresearch.org/social-trends/2019/04/09/race-in-america-2019/.

Kali Pal, Kusum, et al. World Economic Forum, 2022, *Global Gender Gap Report 2022*, https://www3.weforum.org/docs/WEF_GGGR_2022.pdf. Accessed 2022.

"The Labor Market for Recent College Graduates." *Federal Reserve Bank of New York*, 12 Feb. 2021, https://www.newyorkfed.org/research/college-labor-market/college-labor-market_compare-majors.html.

Miller, Stephen. "Unequal Career Advancement Fuels Gender Pay Gap." *SHRM*, 2 Apr. 2019, https://www.shrm.org/resourcesandtools/hr-topics/compensation/pages/unequal-career-advancement-fuels-gender-pay-gap.aspx.

Norton, Michael I., and Samuel R. Sommers. "Whites See Racism as a Zero-Sum Game That They Are Now Losing." *Perspectives on Psychological Science*, vol. 6, no. 3, May 2011, pp. 215–218, doi:10.1177/1745691611406922.

Reiners, Bailey. "57 Diversity in the Workplace Statistics You Should Know." Edited by Hal Kloss, *Built In*, 21 Oct. 2021, https://builtin.com/diversity-inclusion/diversity-in-the-workplace-statistics.

Schaeffer, Katherine. "10 Facts About Today's College Graduates." *Pew Research Center*, Pew Research Center, 12 Apr. 2022, https://www.pewresearch.org/fact-tank/2022/04/12/10-facts-about-todays-college-graduates/#:~:text=In%202021%2C%20full%2Dtime%20workers,the%20Bureau%20of%20Labor%20Statistics.

"The State of Black Women in Corporate America." *Lean In*, 2020, https://leanin.org/research/state-of-black-women-in-corporate-america#!

"This Equal Pay Day, the Wage Gap Widens for Black Women." *In Our Own Voice: National Black Women's Reproductive Justice Agenda*, 15 Mar. 2022, https://blackrj.org/this-equal-pay-day-the-wage-gap-widens-for-black-women/.

"U.S Department of Labor Reaches Conciliation Agreement for $7,000,000 to Resolve Discrimination Allegations." *U.S Department of Labor*, 30 Sept. 2019, https://www.dol.gov/newsroom/releases/ofccp/ofccp20190930-0. Accessed 2022.

"Women Are Paid Less Than Men—and the Gap Is Closing Too Slowly." *Lean In*, 2022, https://leanin.org/equal-pay-data-about-the-gender-pay-gap.

"Women in the Workplace 2021." *Lean In*, 2021, https://leanin.org/women-in-the-workplace-report-2021/how-companies-can-advance-diversity-and-inclusion.

Young, Robin, and Serena McMahon. "Name Discrimination Study Finds Lakisha and Jamal Still Less Likely to Get Hired than Emily and Greg." *WBUR*, 18 Aug. 2021, https://www.wbur.org/hereandnow/2021/08/18/name-discrimination-jobs.

ABOUT THE AUTHORS

MELODY SIMMONS-HUDSON

Melody is the CEO and co-founder of Head Not The Tail Productions (HNTT) and co-founder of The Equal Balance Movement. A movement inspired by the need to advocate for Women's Pay Equality. She is the director of the documentary, *Invisible Women: Being a Black Woman in Corporate America*. Melody currently co-hosts a podcast with Monica Simmons called "The Invisible Women Podcast".

Simmons-Hudson brings 20-plus years as a Corporate America professional and obtained her M.B.A. in Finance from Holy Names University in 2012. Melody is also a Certified Financial Literacy coach (NFEC), and has a passion for empowering underrepresented women and girls to reach their full potential in life. Melody's philanthropy efforts include being a member of Women of Impact leaders: Girls Inc (Oakland, CA), NAACP, and part of the UN-USA community to name a few. Melody continues to lead efforts as an executive strategy consultant to companies in the SF/Bay Area to help organizations foster diverse talent and grow their bottom line.

MONICA SIMMONS

Monica co-founded The Equal Balance Movement and Head Not The Tail Productions. Monica also hosts *The Invisible Women Podcast* for women empowerment on Spotify and Apple podcasts. Monica is a member of the NAACP and BWOPA. She has spoken on panels and held workshops speaking on Black women in the workplace at tech companies and colleges, such as Instacart, Evergreen Valley College, and more. Before producing her first documentary film, *Invisible Women: Being A Black Woman In Corporate America*, Monica worked for more than a decade as a manager within the tech start-up industry in the California Bay area. Noticing the lack of diversity in tech, she became an advocate and obtained Diversity/Equity/Inclusion Certification. Her business/marketing degree allowed her to venture into serial entrepreneurship. Monica lives in the Bay area where she continues to fight for equality for Black women in the workplace.

www.ingramcontent.com/pod-product-compliance
Lightning Source LLC
Chambersburg PA
CBHW062125020426
42335CB00013B/1106